CLARINET ACOUSTICS

CLARINET ACOUSTICS

O. Lee Gibson

Indiana University Press

Bloomington and Indianapolis

This book is a publication of

Indiana University Press
601 North Morton Street
Bloomington, IN   47404-3797   USA

http://www.indiana.edu/~iupress

Telephone orders   800-842-6796
Fax orders   812-855-7931
Orders by email   iuporder@indiana.edu

First paperback edition 1998
© 1994 by O. Lee Gibson

The paper used in this publication meets the minimum
requirements of American National Standard for Information
Sciences—Permanence of Paper for Printed Library Materials,
ANSI Z39.48-1984.

Manufactured in the United States of America

Library of Congress Cataloging-in-Publication Data

Gibson, O. Lee (Oscar Lee)
    Clarinet acoustics / O. Lee Gibson.
        p.   cm.
    Includes bibliographical references and index.
    ISBN 0-253-32576-5 (cloth)
    1. Clarinet—Construction.   2. Music—Acoustics and physics.
I. Title
ML946.G5   1994
788.6'21923—dc20   94-75

ISBN 0-253-21172-7   (paperback)

2   3   4   5   02   01   00   99   98

CONTENTS

v

PREFACE

IN THE PRESENTATION of this volume my goals are to help both clarinetists and clarinet makers better understand the principles which guide the design of the instrument, to suggest means of acoustical enhancement which have not been fully utilized, and to discuss currently existing but rarely available mechanical improvements. My primary concerns are the modal frequency ratios of a clarinet and the timbres of its tones, as well as the instrument's dynamic range, stability, flexibility, and responsiveness.

Every dimension of a wind instrument is related to every other one, whether it be length, volume, size, weight, or material. Much as one might wish to discuss one element without regard to another, such an organization is inappropriate. Therefore, there may be several statements of salient facts as they relate in turn to different acoustical desiderata.

Inspiration for this study could have come from Ivan Mueller, Carl Baermann, Louis-Auguste Buffet, H. Klosé, the Alberts of Brussels, O. Oehler, Henri Selmer, G. Leblanc, Robert Carrée, W. Hans Moennig, or others who have devoted their lives to the betterment of this noble instrument. That it did not is due to the understandable but unfortunate tradition that trade secrets must never be revealed and may even die with the discoverer. How else can one account for the unending vacillation of clarinet bore dimensions which has occurred during the past two centuries?

The model for this book has come from a personal friend and clarinetist who must be ranked as the most important theoretical acoustician of musical wind instruments in the twentieth century, Arthur H. Benade. Although one may not agree with his every conclusion, Benade has led us through the maze of wind instrument theory.

CLARINET ACOUSTICS

1

ACOUSTICAL HISTORY
OF THE CLARINET

ANY INSTRUMENT CALLED a clarinet is less than 300 years old. Cylindrically bored single-reed woodwinds were hardly more than toys in western Europe until the eighteenth century; no such woodwind was described in either Praetorius' *Syntagma Musicum* (1619) or Mersenne's *Harmonie Universelle* (1636–1637). The history of the clarinet, which was singularly obscure in the first half of the eighteenth century, develops rapidly after 1750, as detailed by Rendall, Kroll, Baines, Bate, and others, each from their own geographical viewpoint. The present volume mentions only the most important events and names in that history.

In Mediterranean ports tourists may be offered single- and double-cane pipes, with finger holes and a reed. Matching a mouthpiece and/or a reed to the tube has always been problematical, whether as a toy or a way to make a living! The availability of mass-produced single reeds in the twentieth century has done wonders for the clarinet and the saxophone, allowing us to forget or overlook some advantages of a double-reed generator. The crumhorn of the Renaissance, having an exceedingly narrow bore (ca. 4 mm.) could have been played with a single reed. Indeed, in the twentieth century the oboe and bassoon have been fitted with single-reed mouthpieces when good double reeds were scarce. At school music contests one soon realizes that such equipment may provide only an assured mediocrity.

The Hungarian taragato, a relative of the still-popular Mediterranean oboe, had a checkered history during the nineteenth century, when it appeared successively with oboe, simple clarinet, and saxophone mechanisms, and was played as either a single- or a double-reed instrument. Perhaps the taragato was an important source for Adolphe Sax in developing the instrument to which he gave his name. After this Brussels native had established himself in Paris with a complete family of saxophones, the French bandmaster Sarrus fitted similar instruments with double reeds, calling them sarrusophones. However, modulation of the innate, brassy brilliance of such an instrument's large, unfraised tone holes is more readily accomplished with the single reed.

One should note that, like the taragato, the bassoon, oboe, and saxophone are half-wave instruments because of their conical bore, whereas the flute is a half-wave generator because it is a pipe which is open at both ends.

During the most productive quarter century in the history of woodwind instruments, 1825–1850, Paris was the locale of choice for their important inventors. Theobald Boehm's genius transformed an archaic Baroque holdover, the eight-key reversed-cone flute, into a resplendent successor which has survived nearly one and one-half centuries with only one major mechanical improvement, Briccialdi's B♭ thumb lever. At the same time the Baroque oboe underwent separate developments in Vienna by Sellner and Koch, and in Paris by Brod and Triébert. The Vienna oboe as made by the firm of Zuleger has a regional importance today, while the firm of Triebért's foreman and eventual successor, F. Lorée, has led the way to world-wide dominance by the Conservatory-system oboe. Likewise, the most influential manufacturer of the German-system bassoon has borne the name of Wilhelm Heckel since 1831, while in Paris Louis Auguste Buffet and perhaps his nephew L. Buffet Crampon led in the manufacture of the French-system bassoon, which at the end of the twentieth century is built only by the firm of Buffet Crampon.

The Clarinet in the Eighteenth and Nineteenth Centuries

Apparently the predilection of the clarinet for a single-reed generator was overwhelming from the beginning, since its smaller tone holes and thick walls provided ample means for tonal voicing. The meagre and conjectural subject of the development of the chalumeau and then the clarinet has been a favorite one for clarinet historians, although very little music was composed specifically for the clarinet until about 1740. For our purposes it will suffice to say only that the chalumeau became a clarinet when, under the aegis of J. C. Denner and his sons at Nuremberg, it became capable of producing some semblance of a chromatic scale of nearly four octaves up from a written low E below the treble staff.

Throughout the eighteenth century the commonly used clarinet remained limited to five or six keys, but there were players, such as Anton Stadler, of Vienna, who at the end of Mozart's life played extended-range low-C clarinets in several keys. These instruments, perhaps made by Lotz in Vienna only for Stadler, disappeared along with Mozart's autographs of his Quintet, K. 581, and Concerto, K. 622, during Stadler's rather untrustworthy and dissolute lifetime.

Ivan Mueller's claim in 1812 to have been the first to add seven new keys to the clarinet seems overdrawn. His contribution may more accurately have been that of having chosen the best of the new mechanisms then being tried by players and makers everywhere in Europe. Though rejected by a tradition-bound faculty committee of the Paris Conservatory, which preferred the tones of different clarinets for each key, something close to Mueller's thirteen-keyed model nevertheless became a necessity almost immediately. Adolphe Sax, who was trained as a clarinetist at the Brussels Conservatory, is credited with the subsequent addition of the right-hand finger rings to the Mueller model, as well as the production of an outstanding metal bass clarinet.

The creation of the landmark alternative to the Mueller system also occurred in Paris, when in 1844 Louis Auguste Buffet, prompted by H. Klosé and Theobald Boehm (for each of whom Buffet had crafted instruments), patented his "clarinet with moveable rings." Both Mueller's and Buffet's clarinets have undergone successive generations of improvements, but, unlike Mueller's, which only distantly resembled the present Oehler-system German clarinet, Buffet's original invention is still quite close to what is now called the Boehm clarinet. The Klosé-Buffet Boehm-inspired clarinet was soon followed by oboes and bassoons made by leading Paris craftsmen utilizing Boehm's moveable rings and larger tone holes, but these instruments were almost invariably strident in their tones, and did not succeed.

The Clarinet in the Early Twentieth Century

It is unfortunate that Oskar Oehler's adaptation of the oboe's F resonance mechanism to the Mueller-system clarinet at the beginning of the new century did not find its way around the world until most professional clarinetists had given up the Mueller for the Boehm system. (Alexander [sic] Selmer's New York catalogs of ca. 1920 do in fact show such a model by Henri Selmer.) Not even E. J. Albert's Mueller (Albert System) clarinets could compete with the Boehms, since they lacked the one device which could have brought them to full equality. In the United States the first era of the famous Oehler players concluded with the retirement of Victor Polatschek (Boston Symphony Orchestra), Robert Lindemann (Chicago Symphony Orchestra), and Simeon Bellison (New York Philharmonic Orchestra) about 1950. Since ca. 1975 there has been a revival of the Oehler in the United States with the remarkable clarinets of Herbert Wurlitzer, as played by the likes of Michelle Zukovsky, the daughter of a former Los Angeles Philharmonic principal, Kalman Bloch. (At the end of the century the Oehler-system Wurlitzer is frequently required for auditions in German orchestras.)

Similar acoustical principles apply to all woodwinds, different as a flute or an oboe may be from a clarinet or a bassoon. However, with the stopped-pipe, quarter-wavelength clarinet, dimensional exactitude is twice as critical as with a half-wavelength body. We shall deal here with clarinets in both leading systems and with important variants and expansions of each. Certain features which are common to only one genre might be beneficially adapted for the other, though less than two percent of the world's clarinets are now made in the German system.

Whereas the German clarinet-making establishment has always believed that its players deserve and will purchase every proven mechanical improvement, some of these devices for the Boehm are currently available only from German and, more recently, Japanese makers. For a European player a trip to the maker's atelier may be quick and relatively inexpensive, but for many on other continents that may not be the case. Undoubtedly the contrasting attitudes of the makers in France and Germany, in particular, rest on the way each determines success or failure. Following a now-extended history of worldwide dominance in Boehm clarinet manufacture, French firms concentrate on efficient mass production of a limited number of models whereas a German company may contract to make instruments for a certain person of recognized standing.

The ordinary Boehm is much simpler to make than is the mechanically complex Oehler, which is still evolving, though perhaps less rapidly at present. Excellent mechanical and acoustical options for the Boehm soprano clarinet frequently fall by the wayside or even fail to receive a trial. Changes are difficult for either maker, but for the custom producer they can be done (more expensively, of course) without completely destroying production, and this flexibility has enabled the best German firms to adapt to exceptional requests. However, those that have not reacted well have not survived, and we have therefore a chronic shortage of the best German clarinets, a situation which continues to deter clarinetists from a possible change to the German system, or even to the Reform Boehm.

2

FAMOUS CLARINETISTS AND
THEIR INSTRUMENTS

ARTISTS IN ANY medium must find ways to transcend the limitations and weaknesses of their equipment, and great clarinetists of every period have done so unbelievably well. Many have de-
manded an extension of the resources of their instruments, perhaps
the first being Mozart's clarinetist, Anton Stadler (1753–1812). His
preoccupation with extended-range soprano clarinets is responsible
for their revival in the late twentieth-century. As noted previously,
these instruments were apparently made for him by Lotz of Vienna.
One must believe that this rogue could play like an angel!

Richard Mühlfeld (1856–1907), Brahms's clarinetist of a century
later, whom Brahms discovered late in life and called "meine Pri-
madonna," inspired the semi-retired master to compose for Mühlfeld his four wonderful chamber works (Trio Op. 114, Quintet Op.
115, and Sonatas Op. 120). The eighteen-keyed Mueller-Baermann
system clarinets that belonged to Mühlfeld can be seen at the Staat-
liche Museum in Meiningen, Germany, where he played in the court
orchestra.

Joseph Schreurs (1863–1921), of Brussels and Chicago, whose
business card I found in the case of my ca. 1912 E. J. Albert clarinets,
played (and sold) Albert's 15 mm. Mueller-Albert system instruments, which had beautiful tone and remarkable intonation for such
a relatively large bore. These instruments are notable for the fact
that all their tone holes are bored above the level required to prevent
accumulation of moisture, which still occurs in the tone holes of
Boehm clarinets. Albert's secret of improved pitch in the larger-
bored instrument is that of properly placed, slightly larger, and less-

fraised tone holes. Schreur's Alberts probably lacked Oehler's now standard B♭–F–D resonance vent mechanism (as do mine).

Simeon Bellison (1883–1953), of Russia and New York, became the admired principal clarinetist of the Philharmonic-Symphony Orchestra of New York (following the merger in 1928 of the city's two major orchestras, the Philharmonic Society of New York and the New York Symphony Orchestra). Bellison, also a leading teacher at the Juilliard School, played Oehler and Oehler-system clarinets, although he did not encourage his students to do so. The orchestra which Toscanini inherited produced massive Teutonic tones, including Bellison's, which were at times hardly discernible from those of the bass clarinet in his early years. With age and softer reeds, Bellison became for me an excellent model. Though it is said that he never allowed his pupils to use vibrato, in the radio première of his clarinet and orchestra arrangement of Mozart's *Concert Rondo* (originally for piano and orchestra), Bellison suddenly appeared with a beautifully controlled vibrato! His 15 mm. clarinets, with smaller, more highly fraised tone holes, produced very dark and weighty sounds, although the Buffet Crampon R 13 of the time was of similar bore and fraising.

Gaston Hamelin, 1884–1951, of Paris and Boston, a principal clarinetist in Paris and of the Boston Symphony Orchestra, represented the best of French clarinetists of his time. One of his monuments is a still highly prized recording of Debussy's *Première Rhapsodie* for Clarinet and Orchestra. He performed on the clarinets of Henri Selmer, which during his life were made in bores under 15 mm., with a long reversed cone in the left-hand (LH) joint and barrel and with unfraised tone holes. In my opinion the very best unfraised Selmer clarinets in the Boehm system were made before the Balanced Tone series of about 1934 and in bores ca. 14.85 mm. These were the models Hamelin would have played. Between the World Wars, Selmer's clarinets were by far the most popular professional clarinets throughout the world. (Where are those clarinets now?) I do not know when Henri Selmer abandoned fraising in what had always been, and is again, a fraised soprano clarinet.

Benny Goodman, the greatest clarinetist of the swing era, also assured for the Selmer clarinet its reputation as the clarinet of swing and the big band. Goodman, who had grown up with the Selmer, made only one brief attempt to adapt to the pre-1950, near-15 mm. Buffet Crampon R 13; he used it for his performance of the Copland *Concerto for Clarinet* in Dallas and seemed baffled by this strange (for him) clarinet. Neither the unfraised Selmer nor the larger-bore Buffet Crampon is extant almost a half century later, but they were both notable instruments: the Selmer for its incomparable facility, the Buffet Crampon for its fine tones, but with rather narrow modal ratios.

Daniel Bonade, a remarkable graduate of the Paris Conservatory, became principal clarinetist of the Philadelphia Orchestra and later of the Cleveland Orchestra. He retired to New York City and was regarded as the most famous and revered clarinet teacher in the United States after 1945. His instrument was again the R 13, but with an important distinction: the ca. World War I Buffet Crampon clarinets were made to a somewhat smaller bore than were those sold to aspiring symphony players around 1936 (when I bought mine). The smaller bore made a world of difference, lending ease and facility to Bonade's intonation that most of the rest of us did not have. I once borrowed a much older Buffet Crampon A from Earl Bates, then my student and later principal clarinetist of the St. Louis Symphony—and this A, as Bonade's must have been, was astounding as to both its pitch and its sound. What a loss it was to us all when Buffet Crampon followed the lead of Selmer into enlarged clarinet bores, from perhaps 1925 until Robert Carrée's enlightened 14.65 mm. sopranos appeared in 1950.

Reginald Kell, the celebrated English clarinetist, was a twentieth-century pioneer in the use of vibrato and the first teacher of clarinet at the Aspen Music School. He told us that his clarinets may have been made by the Martel brothers in Paris. I believe they had a bore close to 15 mm. and moderately fraised tone holes.

Quite another model are the clarinets made famous by Frederick Thurston, Jack Brymer, and Gervase de Peyer: the Boosey & Hawkes 1010s, with perhaps the largest bores ever applied to soprano clarinets, about 15.3 mm. I suspect that their instruments had been made to a somewhat smaller size, since my 1969 pair had such incredibly undersized middle twelfths that they could not have been played in any respectable symphony orchestra, even with the more open mouthpiece facings favored by the English. This question has been settled for the present, at least, by the fact that very few soprano clarinets with bores larger than 15 mm. have been made since 1975.

Karl Leister, principal clarinetist of the Berlin Philharmonic, plays instruments made by Herbert Wurlitzer, as required by the orchestra itself, which owns complete sets for every member of the section. After playing an incomparable Wurlitzer Oehler clarinet on the day following the death of Herr Wurlitzer in 1989 at Neustadt/Aisch, I was told that most Wurlitzer soprano clarinets were made to a bore of about 14.7 mm. for a generation or more, having been reduced from the 15 mm. favored by Fritz Wurlitzer. Wurlitzer's Model 100c (Solisteninstrument), made in the keys of A, B♭, and C, was sold in 1989 at a price of DM 8900. The Wurlitzer Reform Boehm, developed by Ernst Schmidt of Mannheim but taken over by members of the Wurlitzer family later in the twentieth century, has had continued usage, particularly in the Netherlands and the British Isles.

In 1994 a majority of clarinetists in the United States continue to favor either the Buffet Crampon 14.65 mm. R 13 soprano clarinets or similar models by leading woodwind instrument makers. Product improvement by Selmer, Leblanc, and Yamaha has greatly increased the choices available to professionals, making it possible for section members to match pitches with instruments of different manufacture, although perhaps another generation of improvement is necessary to bring the clarinet to its acoustical zenith.

3

NATIONAL SCHOOLS OF
CLARINET MANUFACTURE

France

AMONG THE EARLY nineteenth-century makers the name of
Louis Auguste Buffet is most important, since it was he who
developed the so-called Boehm system clarinet, realizing the ideas
posed by H. Klosé for the clarinet with those already developed by
Boehm for the flute. (The history of the emergence of the family-
owned firm of Buffet Crampon is told in a booklet which may obtained from the company.)

During the second half of the nineteenth century Martin Frères,
F. Triébert, A. Robert, Martel Frères, Auguste Buffet, and Marigaux
were active clarinet makers, and most of them continued successfully into the twentieth century. Various members of the Lefebvre
family have distinguished themselves not only as manufacturers of
clarinets but also as performers, composers, and teachers of woodwinds. Much the same may be said of the Leblanc and Noblet families, with Georges Leblanc establishing his firm in 1904.

Frederick C. Selmer, the father of Henri and Alexandre Selmer
(Alexandre anglicized his name in the United States), was the first
clarinetist to receive a gold medal from the Conservatoire National
de Musique of Paris. This information is in Alexander's New York
catalog of about 1919 (undated), which shows not only fully improved Boehm and German systems but also an elaborate plateau
Barret system, all by Henri Selmer. By this time Buffet Crampon
and Selmer were competing on almost equal terms throughout the
world; Leblanc became a strong third after World War II. As Selmer

developed its aggressive marketing of new (but not always better) models in the second quarter of the century while being pushed by the innovations of Georges and Leon Leblanc, smaller French makers gradually disappeared, and even Buffet Crampon was threatened by the aftermath of the German occupation. Its severe financial crisis was resolved after 1950 by a successful introduction of smaller-bored soprano clarinets made by factory manager Robert Carrée, which he called "polycylindrical."

Belgium

In Brussels through the last half of the nineteenth century and the first quarter of the twentieth, the Mahillon and Albert families were among the most important clarinet makers of the world. The founder of the Albert dynasty was Eugene, whose sons Jacques, E. J., and J. B. exported large numbers of both German (called Albert system in the United States) and Boehm clarinets. Among the last Brussels makers was Jacques Lucien Albert, whose rosewood Boehm clarinets were beautifully played by my teacher, R. M. Arey, in 1940.

Germany

The most influential German clarinet maker of the twentieth century has been Oskar Oehler (at first a member of the Berlin Philharmonic), whose clarinets have been the models for all German-system makers since about 1910. Other leaders have been Ernst Schmidt of Mannheim (best known as the inventor of the Reform Boehm), Fritz Graessel of Nuremberg, the firm of Wilhelm Heckel at Biebrich-am-Rhein (whose catalog lists many optional mechanisms for both German and Boehm clarinets), and F. A. Uebel of Markneukirchen (who developed the final version of Oehler's $B\flat$-F-D resonance mechanism). Since perhaps 1940 new standards for the German clarinet have been set by Fritz Wurlitzer, by other family members, and particularly by Herbert Wurlitzer at Neustadt/Aisch (d. 1989). My own Oehler-system $B\flat$ is excellently bored, by Hans

Kreul of Tübingen, but lacks the now standard thumb-key low E and F resonance vents.

Austria

Since about 1950 the Hammerschmidt family of Wattens has made the German-system clarinets played in the Vienna Philharmonic. While they follow the Oehler model, they are acoustically different, being of somewhat larger bores than those of the revised Herbert Wurlitzer model of 14.7 mm., now the standard in Germany, and they therefore have somewhat less need for the Wurlitzer low E and F resonance vents.

Great Britain

British clarinet making had a long and fruitful history, but the profession suffered the effects of increasing competition from mass production by the leading French firms. The one important surviving maker in Britain, Boosey & Hawkes, closed its production of first-line clarinets in England after it purchased Buffet Crampon & Cie. about 1983. For some time the English firm's clarinets had been adrift without knowledgeable direction, judging by my own purchase of first a set of 1010s about 1970 and then a set of their 15 mm. instruments in 1979, none of which could be played in tune. A select group of custom makers exists.

Japan

The fourth quarter of the twentieth century has seen the rise of the Japanese conglomerate Yamaha to a position of equality with the leading French firms in its manufacture of Boehm clarinets. Current production also includes Yamaha's German Boehm, which is comparable to—though not identical with—the Wurlitzer Reform Boehm.

China

Having begun in imitation of the large-bored British clarinets of a generation ago, the use of contemporary 14.65 mm. models is still in its infancy, although another decade will almost certainly see the beginning of Chinese or Taiwanese exports of Western wind instruments.

Chile

Luis Rossi, of Los Leones #79 Dep. 36, Santiago 9, Chile, deserves mention as almost the last fine custom maker of soprano clarinets in the world. He makes beautiful one-piece clarinets (without a center joint, which greatly improves $C_{\sharp}$–$G_{\sharp}$–F pitches), in a 15 mm. English bore or a smaller French bore, with a choice of blackwood or rosewood.

The Netherlands

While at the beginning of the twentieth century German-system clarinets were in a majority, at its end one finds both Wurlitzer Reform Boehms and Oehlers in the leading orchestras. This diversity seems to be representative of the country as a whole, with German-made clarinets predominating.

Italy and Spain

At mid-century, orchestral clarinetists frequently used only one extended-range instrument, as still may be seen and heard at Milan's La Scala. The full-improved Selmer, a favorite of theatre orchestra players around the world, is still popular. In Italy, Rampone and Orsi clarinets have been widely used.

Scandinavia

Though Danish, Swedish, Norwegian, and Finnish clarinetists formerly used German-system clarinets, the Boehm clarinet is now predominant. Carl Nielsen's wonderful *Concerto for Clarinet and Orchestra* (1928) was written for his close friend Aage Oxenvad, who played Boehm clarinets.

Central Europe and the Russian Republics

The transition to the Boehm clarinet among professional clarinetists was gradually completed in the quarter century after World War I, although in 1967 the principal clarinetist of the Leningrad Philharmonic still played the Oehler. As is generally true elsewhere, professionals use first-line French instruments.

United States

Student-line instruments are made by Mexican workers for sale in the United States by companies which have transferred their plants across the border. In the first half of the century there was a thriving, if not quite distinguished, industry of clarinet manufacture of instruments of higher quality in the United States. The longest-lasting of these first-line firms were Penzel-Mueller and Conn, the latter still an important maker of brass instruments. Between the two World Wars the metal clarinet was popular, and a host of band-instrument firms made them as well as some wood, ebonite, plastic, and impregnated plywood clarinets. Among the clarinet makers were William S. Haynes (the renowned flute maker, who made perhaps the only solid silver clarinets ever sold), Cundy-Bettoney, Harry Bettoney, Harry Pedler, H. N. White, Holton, Harry O'Brien, Henry Gunckel, Pan-American, and Jan Williams. None of these firms could withstand the competition of the large French factories, located in the countryside away from Paris, where their workers can bicycle to work.

Australia and New Zealand

Following colonial traditions, until recently most of the best musicians of these countries were trained in Britain and returned with French or English instruments; now their clarinets are French or Japanese.

Africa

African wood is shipped to Europe, where it is variously stored (sometimes, as in 1967, in bags outside the Buffet Crampon factory), and eventually returned as clarinets!

4

THE EAR AS AN ANALYZER
OF MUSICAL TONES

THE DEVELOPMENT AND near perfection of electronically synthesized musical instruments leads one to question the future of traditional acoustical instruments and the organizations in which they are used. Undoubtedly, synthesizers will become more capable of producing some of the subtleties of our orchestras, chamber ensembles, and soloists, but at this time one cannot predict an obsolescence of acoustical musical instruments.

The human capacity for discrimination of pitches is a natural talent which can be developed with practice but has innate limitations. Keenness centers in the pitches of the treble staff, falling off in the octave above it as well as below the bass staff. These decreases of acuity at the extremes of the frequency spectrum are made less serious by the capacity to adjust pitches by the elimination of beats.

Less has been published about how well the ear can analyze musical tones. The following is the abstract of an article that appeared in *The Clarinet* 5/2 (1978):7:

The Ear as an Analyzer of Musical Tones. O. Lee Gibson and Dennis A. Guillaume, School of Music, North Texas State University, Denton, Texas 76203.—Plomp and Mimpen (1968) found the ear able to hear separately the first five to seven harmonic partials of tones in monaural tests. Duifhuis (1970) reported that a harmonic as high as the twentieth may be perceived separately. In the present tests, oscillators were phase-locked and adjusted to a uniform A-weighted sound level. The resultant complex tone could be deprived of any thus-amplified partial by means of an electronic switch. In binaural listening to a two-element loudspeaker in a music room, experienced musicians were able to duplicate the frequency of any partial as high as the twelfth for 44-Hz tones, the fifteenth for 62.5-Hz tones, the fourteenth for 125-Hz tones, the eleventh for 250-Hz tones, the eighth for 500-Hz tones, and the fifth for 1000-Hz tones. In dichotic listening to a tone having the same phase in both ears the capability was frequently reduced by 10% to 25%.

As with pitch acuity, the ear's capacity to identify separately partials of a tone falls off rapidly at the extremes of the audible frequencies. Also, presbycusis, the loss of capacity to hear high frequencies, increases with advancing age, particularly in men. Though such losses are real, they seldom interfere with our recognition and appreciation of instrumental timbres in music.

Frequency Analysis of Clarinet Tones

Among musical instruments, clarinets and closed organ pipes have the most consistent and recognizable spectra. Clarinet spectra show almost without exception an appreciable odd-partial predominance from the lowest tones through written top-line F, regardless of the pitch of the instrument itself. Above this tone the partials fall off more and more uniformly, so that the written C above the staff has no vestige of odd-partial predominance. Yet the ear still almost infallibly tells one that this sound is that of a clarinet. (Tones in this range and above may also be recognized in part by noises of attack and reed vibration.) The same may be said of the ear's differentiation of oboe, violin, saxophone, or viola tones, which may have spectra that cannot be identified by formulae, but only by the ear, as is also true of the clarinet's third-mode tones.

Aside from their odd-partial predominance, a most notable characteristic of clarinet tones is their striking correlation of dynamic level with harmonic complexity. As John Backus has written:

> When the clarinet is blown softly, the reed does not touch the mouthpiece; its motion is nearly sinusoidal. . . . When the blowing pressure is increased to produce loud tones, the reed is in contact

with the mouthpiece for a little more than half the cycle. . . . Air is then admitted into the mouthpiece in short bursts, and the air flow is a mixture of a steady (average) flow plus a complex vibration in which all of the harmonics of the fundamental frequency are present. [*The Acoustical Foundations of Music*, 2d ed. (New York: W. W. Norton & Co., 1977), p. 239.]

Does a clarinet have prominent formant ranges? (A formant has been defined as a region of frequencies which may be emphasized, regardless of the location of a fundamental frequency.) Somewhat similar to the d'amoré bell of the English horn, but effective over a wider range of fundamental frequencies, is the unique polycylin-drical reaming of the LH joint which occurred in the Buffet Cram-pon R 13 after 1949. It is responsible for the distinctive formant emphasis which many players believe they hear and feel in this clarinet's tones. The fact that such a formant is apparently more easily heard than detected through spectral analysis is further support for the ear's superiority as an analyzer of sounds. Concerning clarinet formants: If the flute is in fact the soprano of the orchestral woodwind section and the oboe is its mezzo soprano, isn't the soprano clarinet more often than not its contralto? Perhaps it is both a soprano and a contralto.

5

PRINCIPLES FOR THE ACOUSTICAL
DESIGN OF THE CLARINET

IN THE TWENTIETH century, as before, manufacturers of musical instruments have usually operated in an empirical world of cut and try rather than the theoretical one of acoustical science. Nevertheless, during this time (especially in France), there have been collaborations in experiments supported jointly by government and industry, and in the United States the National Science Foundation has occasionally sponsored scientific research in music and musical instruments at academic institutions. As one might expect, the emphasis in France has usually been on reporting experiments, while in the United States the elucidation of derived theoretical principles has often resulted.

Excellent sources for acoustical principles in English are the publications of the scientists Arthur H. Benade (a practiced clarinetist) and John Backus (a bassoonist in chamber ensembles). However, the reader must still make a useful extraction and organization of these principles as they apply to a particular instrument.

> Woodwind musical instruments, like the brasses, have a flow control-device (the reed valve), the function of which is to alter the rate at which air enters the mouthpiece. . . . Woodwinds also make use of an air column whose natural frequencies must be properly arranged to set up regimes of oscillation in conjunction with the reed valve. . . . Preserving a constant frequency ratio between the vibrational modes as the holes . . . are opened is essential in all woodwinds and provides a limitation on the types of air column (often referred to as the bore) that are useful. [Arthur H. Benade, *Fundamentals of Musical Acoustics*, pp. 430–31.]

Terminology for the Bore

A localized enlargement or diminution in a wind instrument's bore is called a "perturbation." Its purpose is to correct (to the extent possible) imperfect ratios which can occur between the frequencies of two, three, or more harmonic modes. Perturbations also affect the timbres of tones which pass through the perturbed area, as in the bell of an English horn or the mouthpiece, barrel, reversed cone, lower flare, and bell of a clarinet. The air column is enclosed by the bore and its closed holes.

Terminology for a Stopped Pipe

While the reed valves of oboes, bassoons, saxophones, and clarinets perform similarly (no matter whether they are single or double), the conical bores of the first three provide a pressure node at or near each end of the tube in its first vibrational mode, furnishing a complete set of overblown harmonic modes. Because the clarinet acts as a closed cylindrical pipe when its reed valve closes against the mouthpiece at one-half wavelength (there having been an impulse of large pressure amplitude, variously called a "pressure loop" or an "amplitude loop," generated by the reed valve at the beginning of its cycle), the original condensation is reflected as a rarefaction at the pressure node at the effective end of the tube. (The pressure node is characterized as the point of maximum oscillatory flow.) When the rarefaction has returned to the closed reed it is reflected as a rarefaction, then reflected at the pressure node as a condensation, finishing its two half-wavelength phases as it reaches the now-open reed. The tube of the clarinet therefore acts as a quarter-wavelength resonator, with approximately one-half of the tubing which the (also cylindrical but open) pipe of the flute must have.

The pressure node in a woodwind will not occur at the first open hole, nor will it occur at the actual termination of the tube; rather, the real node occurs following the complete decompression of its wave impulse, which is dependent on the size of the bore, the size of the open holes, and the mode involved. For the second mode of the clarinet this end effect, or open hole length correction, will be triple that of the first mode, and, for the third mode, five times that of the first mode. Beyond the soprano clarinet's upper third mode, however, end-effect correction becomes so large that all fingerings require alteration or additional venting. (The bass clarinet has exceptional harmonic fingerings.)

The total of all areas enclosed within the bore at a given instant by the mouthpiece, reed, tube, tone holes, pads, and fingers determines the effective area of its bore. With a free embouchure and/or a soft reed, a bore is also effectively larger, so that these factors lower the upper mode frequencies by increasing amounts, as clarinetists already know from common experiences.

Terminology for the Mouthpiece

Though this terminology is not completely standardized, the terms used here are readily identified. We use the term "facing" to include both a curved upper portion or "lay," against which the reed beats, and a lower portion, the sometimes flat and sometimes concave "table," against which the reed is bound. "Window" describes the generally rectangular aperture in the beak, over which the reed vibrates and through which the "windway" (sometimes called "chamber") directs its vibrating air column into the "bore," which is the slightly conical cylinder of the remaining three-fifths of the mouthpiece. The portions of the facing which surround the window are the table, two "side rails," and the "tip rail." The four walls of the windway are the "short wall," the two "side walls," and the "baffle." (The last term stems from one of its dictionary definitions, "an obstruction for deflecting the flow of gases.")

6

BODY MATERIALS
Density and Weight, Finish, and Formants

NOT MUCH TIME needs to be spent here since most of the important decisions in materials for clarinets were made for us long ago. Nor do I intend to question these choices; I wish only to clarify how much wood of a certain quality should be used in a clarinet of a certain pitch.

Density and Weight

We refer here to fibral density (fineness and closeness of fibers, as well as weight per unit of volume). To achieve what is generally agreed to be a tone of the most satisfactory timbre and breadth, a dense, close-textured African, South American, or oriental blackwood (which may have been dark brown before dyeing) has long been preferred. No matter what its name may be in a given country—ebony (*ebené*), grenadilla, Dalberg's blackwood (*Dalbergia melanoxylon*), rosewood, or cocus—it should be knot-free, fine grained, and capable of taking and maintaining a high polish. Boxwood, the instrument makers' early choice, fails in these qualities, although cracks from cold and moisture were less troublesome in boxwood. Cocus and rosewood supply more resonance than does boxwood, though they are lighter than the blackwoods. (Selmer has used rosewood for its E♭ contra altos; during the nineteenth and early twentieth centuries it was much used for soprano clarinets.) The very light boxwood instruments usually have rather neutral tones, which blend well with the limited dynamics of Baroque keyboard and orchestral instruments.

The physicist's definition of density (mass per unit of volume) is important in a woodwind, for it and the quality of an instrument's inner surfaces determine not only timbre but also energy losses in the walls. The player's judgment of, and reaction to, the tones of an instrument are of the greatest importance, though the opinion of a listener, clarinetist or not, will be less critical, as numerous well-documented blindfold tests have proven.

When metal clarinets were replacing those of wood (about 1925), many players in the United States thought that the tones produced by the soft nickel silver body of the Cundy-Bettoney clarinet were superior to those of the brass-bodied Selmer, though the soft metal of the Cundy-Bettoney keys proved to be disastrous. For a concert of the U.S. Army Band in 1930, the clarinet section was fully equipped with this instrument. The section had a marvelously clear and well-colored tone, which was most appropriate to its violinistic role in the wind bands of the time. Why then is the metal clarinet now only a curiosity, at least for pitches higher than those of the bass clarinet? The one quite valid reason is that it remained intractable to the process of fraising (although one maker adopted reversed-conical tone holes). The most widely used bass clarinets (those of Selmer) have possibly never been fraised, and there is no valid reason why Adolphe Sax's metal instruments should have been the first and almost the last.

Clarinets of ebonite and similar compounds, such as ABS plastic, have had their advocates, especially among well-known English players of the past. (Actually, German wooden clarinets with their ebonite tone hole inserts far outlast the wooden tone holes of French clarinets.) However, to be acoustically good, an ebonite wind instrument must be precisely milled after molding; thus it will not have a significant price advantage over a wooden one. In 1982, when I played a very fine milled ebonite clarinet made by Leblanc, the one I ordered was never delivered. Apparently the maker decided that that model could not be sold profitably.

In the years following World War II, the band instrument maker Pan-American tried such materials as laminated, impregnated plywoods, and now ABS plastics are being used not only for barrels and bells but also for the complete instrument. At this point in the clarinet's history, however, our presumption is that as long as fine wood is available it will be the preferred material.

What does it matter to the performer that listeners (even clarinetists) are unable to identify the material when they cannot see it? Although Benade has dismissed the vibration of a wooden clarinet as occurring at such a minuscule level as to render it insignificant, it seems to be a very important factor to the player, and the risk of cracking is actually much lower for a clarinet than for the thick-walled, small-bored upper joint of the oboe. (F. Lorée's milled ebonite oboe sells for a bit more than the wooden model.)

Dimensional and Material Needs for the Body of a Clarinet

In summary, material variants are mass density (weight per unit of volume), fibral structure (whether close-grained or porous), and uniformity of structure (the presence of knots or sapwood, etc.).

The following sample weights of several clarinets having excellent tones are given without regard to the percentages of total weight invested in the body or the keys. All are made of (presumably, African) blackwood:

Buffet Crampon, 14.65 mm.	B♭:	723 gr., 25.5 oz.
	A:	744 gr., 26.25 oz.
Selmer Recital, 14.4 mm.	B♭:	801 gr., 28.25 oz.
	A:	822 gr., 29 oz.
H. Kreul, Oehler, 14.7 mm.	B♭:	708 gr., 24.9 oz.
E. J. Albert, Mueller, 15 mm.	B♭:	638 gr., 22.5 oz.

From these specifications we can draw the following conclusions:

1. The E♭, D, C, B♭, and A clarinets are weight adjusted: each lower-pitched instrument weighs more than its upper neighbor.

2. There is an inverse correlation between the size of the bore and its weight: the larger the bore, the less it weighs. This is also true, of course, if the exterior diameters of two clarinets of differ-

ent inner bores are made equal. But if we measure the exteriors of the much smaller-bored Selmer Recital clarinets (which must accordingly be a bit shorter in length), we find that they have the largest exterior diameters as well as greater weight.

3. Adjusting the weight of the clarinet body can affect the timbres of its tones in an important way. In 1812 a Paris Conservatory faculty committee disapproved of Ivan Mueller's clarinet for all keys, but not even a clarinetist always knows which one is being played. The present study does make this point: If there is one best color for a clarinet of a certain pitch, it will be better approximated in a small-bored instrument with additional weight and in a large-bored instrument of less than average weight.

7

PITCH STANDARDS
The Century, the Country, and the Atmosphere

UNFORTUNATELY, IN SPITE of a supposed agreement in 1939 on an international standard of A = 440 Hz, the musical world has yet to resolve completely regional and national pitch differences. These discrepancies have persisted since the last century, when fine early-eighteenth-century stringed instruments had to be refitted with stronger bassbars to accommodate higher string tensions. After 1850 there were still at least three quite different pitch standards at which wind instrument manufacturers had to build their instruments: A = ca. 440 Hz; German high pitch, A = ca. 455 Hz; and French low pitch, A = 435 Hz. In 1994 Germany and Austria still build their woodwinds at 445 Hz, with symphony orchestras in most European countries and some in the United States tacitly preferring to let their pitch rise two or three Hz above a 440 Hz standard. In such situations clarinets often have to be retuned. (For French clarinetists Buffet Crampon usually tunes instruments, such as the Prestige clarinet, to 442 Hz.)

Some woodwind performers and teachers are unaware of the vacillating pitch standards of the twentieth century. Among orchestral players these events seriously concern only organists, percussionists, and woodwind players. However, unsuspecting parents and even teachers may still encounter 435 Hz and 455 Hz woodwinds. (In 1935 I bought in a pawnshop a lovely 435 Hz Triébert A, and quite recently a teacher brought to me a Buffet Crampon B♭ with puzzling pitch problems. It was in fact a 435 Hz clarinet, one which can hardly be properly tuned to 440 Hz; when the tube is shortened sufficiently its upper vents are far too large.)

Atmosphere: Temperature, Humidity, and Altitude

While a rise in temperature slightly lowers frequencies of stringed instruments, it appreciably raises those of wind instruments. Woodwinds with finger holes suffer distortions of intonation as adjustments of length are made. Particularly in a thick-walled clarinet it is important that gaps in its bore should be kept to a minimum by changing barrel lengths and/or using tuning rings. Clarinetists should expect that the usually lower temperatures at higher altitudes will require a slightly shorter instrument.

Since the air column produced by performers always enters a wind pipe with high relative humidity and temperature, frequencies in the lower half of the tube will be most affected when playing at higher altitudes. Because of reduced atmospheric pressure at high altitudes, a single-reed player will need slightly softer reeds. An altitude of two kilometers might require a reduction of one-half grade in reed strength, as compared with that needed at sea level. Emitted tones will accordingly be slightly less voluminous, and frequencies will be lower by as much as one or two cents per kilometer increase in altitude.

8

THE BORE
Cylindrical Diameter, Effective Bore Size, and Modal Ratios

THEOBALD BOEHM, THE son of a German goldsmith, became a flutist in the Munich court orchestra in 1818 and established a factory in 1828, at first for an improved Baroque flute. Nicholson, a London flutist, is credited with a larger, more-cylindrical bore for which Boehm developed his most ingenious mechanism of rings, pads, and keys in the factory of Louis-Auguste Buffet in Paris ca. 1837. However, it remained for Boehm to perfect in 1847 at his own factory a parabolic head joint for a cylindrical body with almost uniformly large tone holes.

Had Boehm been a clarinetist he might have saved a century in the clarinet's acoustical development! Fortunately, his inventions did inspire Buffet and a clarinet professor at the Paris Conservatory, Hyacinthe Klosé (who may be more famous for his own clarinet method), to develop and patent a "clarinet with moveable rings" in 1844. To distinguish it from Ivan Mueller's well-established thirteen-keyed clarinet, they apparently gave it Boehm's name.

Having begun with small bores so that the fingers could easily cover the tone holes, the clarinet (like other woodwinds) was able to produce more pleasant and expressive tones as keys were added to cover larger tone holes in larger bores. During the eighteenth century, soprano clarinet bores were progressively enlarged from diameters of ca. 14 mm. to as much as 15 mm. in Mueller's thirteen-keyed clarinets of 1812. However, during the nineteenth century some makers (including Buffet Crampon) continued to prefer soprano clarinet bores of less than 15 mm. because of their better-sized middle twelfths.

In the twentieth century, fashion again turned to 15 mm. Boehm-system soprano clarinet bores, following Henri Selmer's highly successful unfraised models. (But Buffet Crampon's were less successful because their smaller, fraised tone holes, coupled with an essentially cylindrical bore, produced smaller twelfths.) Boosey & Hawkes's 15.3 mm. 1010s ended a cycle of excess brought to a halt by Robert Carrée's radically innovative 14.65 mm. R 13 sopranos for Buffet Crampon in 1950. Why couldn't Boosey & Hawkes have learned from the past and saved the English clarinet industry? Sheer acoustical incompetence.

Dimensions and Harmonic Modal Ratios

The central, most important principle for the design of wind instruments is the inverse relationship between the size of a bore and the size of its first-mode to overblown-mode ratios. On this subject we find misleading information couched in confused terminology: "With the hole dimensions now customary, wide bores tend to sharpen harmonics and to make others refractory, notably the fifth" (Rendall, *The Clarinet*, p. 43). In reference to high F: "The partial [*sic*] tends to flatness in the case of small bore clarinets, and to sharpness in the larger bore instruments" (Brymer, *Clarinet*, p. 73).

The problems cited here relate to specific instruments, and they are not due to the size of a bore, *per se*, but to tone hole location, sizing, and fraising, and to perturbations of bore. In the most widely used clarinet of the second half of the twentieth century, the Buffet Crampon R 13, the lower-pitched standard high F fingering is caused by the higher placement of its vent (done for the purpose of improving the long, closed high F?), coupled with the polycylindrical reaming of the upper third of its bore at a point which brings down the pitches of its upper third-mode tones.

The large-bored clarinet referred to by Rendall (and Bate) and Brymer is Brymer's B. & H. 1010. Actually, the 1010 is no longer with us simply because its first and second modes produced insufficient modal separation (a sharp first mode with a flat second mode, particularly in its middle twelfths). At the end of the twentieth century the largest soprano clarinet bores, near 15 mm., are frequently chosen by jazz players, who may also use an open mouthpiece facing.

Theoretical Considerations

In his article "On Woodwind Bores," Benade gives a formula (adapted from one by F. M. Morse) for determining the frequency of a normal mode of a nearly cylindrical pipe. Benade's "On the Mathematical Theory of Woodwind Finger Holes" is equally valuable, and for the mathematically competent these two articles are the best available theoretical treatises on woodwind instruments. The applications of Benade's formulae are nevertheless quite difficult, not only because of the minute perturbations of bore usually found in clarinets but also because of the successively enlarged and irregularly fraised tone holes, which may be open or closed. Benade's equations and statements of principle therefore serve best to justify observed acoustical behavior, as does the following:

> a tube whose cross section decreases away from the closed end has a lower fundamental frequency than a uniform pipe, and its normal mode frequencies are spaced more widely than the 1, 3, 5 . . . sequence of the uniform pipe. ["On Woodwind Instrument Bores," p. 139.]

One might expect, then, that a bore which actually does decrease down to the launching of the flare—which is necessary to reduce the oversized lowest twelfths of the clarinet—would be a useful means of enlarging the twelfths of the right-hand finger holes. Has anyone ever seen such a clarinet? (No, only such a Baroque flute.) Instead, even the best of our clarinets with long reversed cones have a cylindrical lower joint bore, one which is actually increased by the ever-enlarging and heavily fraised tone holes. The primary means of producing suitable twelfths from the right-hand finger holes has been to reduce the bore of the clarinet's middle third, in part to compensate for the enlarged tone holes.

9

BORE PERTURBATIONS
Modal Ratios of Differently Sized Cylinders

AN ACOUSTICAL JUSTIFICATION for departures from a strictly cylindrical clarinet bore was first proposed by Lord Rayleigh in the nineteenth century and was recently amplified by Benade. This principle supports the now-flourishing practice of adjusting frequency ratios of the vibrational modes of a wind instrument:

> A localized enlargement of the cross section of an air column (a) lowers the natural frequency of any mode having a large pressure amplitude (and therefore small flow) at the position of the enlargement, and (b) raises the natural frequency of any mode having a pressure node (and therefore large flow) at the position of the enlargement. [Benade, *Fundamentals of Musical Acoustics*, p. 474.]

While application of this principle does not offer complete solutions to modal mistunings caused by the opening of one or more speaker vents (which are controlled to the extent possible by moving the vents and adjusting their sizes), it is useful in predicting and explaining the alterations of modal ratios in clarinets caused by departures from a strict cylinder of a given minimum size. Momentarily disregarding the windway of the mouthpiece and the end-tube flare, which have their own rather firm requirements, we describe here the effects of typical and atypical departures from the clarinet's cylinder:

1. The Mouthpiece: A quasi-cylindrical enlargement of its upper

bore will slightly increase all ratios, with maximal emphasis on the topmost ratios of the upper (fifth and fourth) modes. Conical enlargement of its lower bore maximally increases fourth- and third-mode ratios.

2. The Barrel: Reverse-conical enlargement at the top of the barrel maximally increases third-mode ratios. Cylindrical enlargement of the barrel increases third- and upper second-modes.

3. Upper Half of the Left-Hand Joint: A small-bored reverse-conical barrel on a LH joint having an enlarged, nonlinear reverse-conical upper bore decreasing to its central cylindrical bore at its halfway point increases modal ratios with emphasis upon the middle tones of the second mode; for example, the Selmer 10S, ca. 1990. Alternatively, a moderately sized cylindrical barrel leading through a reversed cone into an intermediate cylinder, which summarily reduces into its central cylinder (unlike any previous design), treats its modal ratios quite individually: Its barrel slightly enlarges most ratios; its second cylinder summarily enlarges middle second-mode twelfths and reduces all but the lowest third-mode ratios, while providing to a smaller bore a rare mellowness of tones. Examples of this construction are the Buffet Crampon R 13, from ca. 1950; to a slightly lesser extent the Yamaha first-line clarinets, from ca. 1980; and the Leblanc first-line clarinets, from ca. 1990. (See Table I, col. a.)

4. The Barrel and the LH Joint: An essentially linear reversed cone, diminishing almost uniformly from the top of the barrel to the center joint, increases all of its modal ratios rather uniformly. The best examples are Herbert Wurlitzer's ca. 14.7 mm. Oehler-system and Reform Boehm clarinets, ca. 1975; and Henri Selmer's pre-1930 ca. 14.85 mm. unfraised Boehms. (This regimen, enhanced only by a slightly smaller-bored reverse-conical barrel, may be the first choice for the soprano Boehm clarinet, as it is for the Oehler system.)

Alternatively, a smaller-bored mouthpiece, a very small-bored reverse-conical barrel, and a massively enlarged, linearly diminishing, full-length reverse-conical LH joint leading into perhaps the smallest cylinder used for a 440 Hz B♭ clarinet in two centuries, ca. 14.40 mm., have been adjoined to produce, with walls of greater thickness, excellent modal ratios and pleasant timbres. An example is the Selmer Recital Series clarinets, ca. 1990. (See Table I, col. b.)

Each of the devices listed here is least effective in adjusting the lower twelfths; the percentage of adjustability gradually diminishes to a point of just noticeable effect. Alterations of modal ratios by graduated bore changes may be predicted by the application of the Rayleigh-Benade principle, but when changes are specifically applied to small portions of a bore, such as a polycylindrical constriction in the LH joint, these perturbations can produce unique changes of ratios as well as timbres. Although a valid judgment of the total effect of Selmer's previously unprecedented venturi bores (different versions of which are found in each of its soprano clarinet models) can only be made after an extended trial, one suspects that in the Recital clarinet's massive offset with a linear diminution to a very small cylinder the instrument may accept a smaller volume of wind.

Subtle perturbation of a clarinet's bore is an art chiefly of the second half of the twentieth century which has not yet seen perfection. I believe that all the designs listed here for Boehm clarinets are transitional and may ultimately be replaced by a more consensual model.

Modal Ratios of Differently Sized Cylinders

If one considers clarinets of different bore diameters which have similar placements of tone holes, similar fraising, and similar departures from a cylinder, one can quite accurately predict the size of at least one twelfth which will be encountered on each instrument, B♭–F, which is nearest the mid-point null at which opening the speaker vent has no effect on the size of the twelfth. The sizes of each of the remaining twelfths may vary considerably with different placements and sizes of the speaker vent.

In this test we chose instruments with cylindrical diameters which differed at the mid-point by almost exactly 0.3 mm.:

Clarinet	Bore	Size of B-F Twelfth
1. Selmer, Recital Series	14.4 mm.	+2 cents
2. Selmer, Series 10 G	14.71 mm.	-1 cent
3. E. J. Albert, Albert System	15.0 mm.	-3 cents
4. Boosey & Hawkes 1010	15.3 mm.	-6 cents

1. Selmer, Recital Series (1987), with its custom, small-bored mouthpiece, a very small Moennig reverse-conical barrel, an exaggerated reverse-conical LH joint, diminishing linearly over its entire length, and a right-hand (RH) cylinder of about 14.4 mm. The Recital B♭, unlike the early A which accompanied it but has since been much improved, is remarkably well tuned. Selmer, which pioneered especial perturbations of lower-joint flare to minimize oversizing of the lowest twelfths, later applied these to the Recital A.

2. Selmer, Series 10 G (1987), with a conventionally bored mouthpiece, a relatively small Moennig-bored barrel, an exaggerated reverse-conical LH joint diminishing nonlinearly over its upper half, and the middle third of its bore about 14.71 mm. This is a revised and greatly improved model of the 1968 Selmer-Gigliotti-Moennig 10 G.

3. E. J. Albert, Albert System (about 1912), with a larger reverse-conical barrel diminishing to a linear 15 mm. bore throughout both joints. As with all Mueller, Albert, Oehler, and Reform Boehm clarinets (which have double venting for the low G–D), flare is delayed at the lower end of the RH joint. With the exception of its unfortunate lack of the Oehler-Uebel forked B♭–F–D resonance vent mechanism, the Albert's twelfths are still very good; it has larger, better-located tone holes with little enough fraising to provide well-sized twelfths.

4. Boosey & Hawkes 1010 (1970), with its very large bore, almost cylindrical mouthpiece, and an absolutely linear 15.3 mm. cylinder throughout its bore down to the launching of its flare. I believe that Thurston's, Brymer's, and De Peyer's earlier 1010s must have been made with a somewhat smaller bore than were my pair from 1970.

We can conclude from this test that, given a particular location, sizing, and fraising of a tone hole at the mid-point null in the otherwise drastic enlargement of a clarinet's twelfths when its speaker vent is opened, the frequency ratio of its first and second modes at this point is fully dependent on the volume enclosed in the central third of the bore.

10

VARIATIONS ON A REVERSED CONE
The Left-Hand Joint

THERE ARE FOUR general types of clarinet bores:

1. Perhaps the oldest type, which was very popular for all clarinets at the turn of the twentieth century, is the strictly cylindrical tube below a reverse-conical barrel. Although this bore was more satisfactory when applied to Mueller, Albert, and Oehler clarinets, which have neither the Boehm's excessively vented upper E–B nor its poorly vented middle-finger B–F$\sharp$, it was used in many Boehms until after 1975. As we have noted, the Boosey & Hawkes 1010 made no use whatsoever of a reversed cone. Until Leblanc made its first smaller-bored clarinets, its instruments were all cylindrical below a reverse-conical barrel.

2. The next oldest (or perhaps the oldest if it was a descendant of the recorder) includes an almost strictly linear reversed cone, which tapers from the top of the barrel through most, if not all, of the LH joint. The most successful clarinets of the first half of the twentieth century, by Henri Selmer, all had such a linear reversed cone. Presumably Fritz or Herbert Wurlitzer adopted this plan either before or with their post–World War II reduction in bore sizes, and by 1970 possibly all German makers had followed suit.

3. In 1949, Robert Carrée, factory manager for Buffet Crampon since 1938, found that if three successively reducing cylinders were substituted for a single, longer reversed cone in the barrel and LH joint of a smaller-bored soprano clarinet, the instrument could produce mellower tones while preserving most, if not all, of the better modal frequency ratios of clarinets having smaller bores. This innovation is present in the R 13 B$\flat$ soprano of 1950, which Carrée called

"polycylindrical," and which has remained essentially unchanged in this model through 1993. (See Table I, col. a.)

Below a cylindrical barrel, at the top of the LH joint, there is a reversed conical reduction into a second, longer cylinder, which ends with an abrupt reduction into the central cylinder of the middle third of the clarinet's bore. In Carrée's R 13 A the three cylinders are differently arranged, with the barrel again being the largest, followed by a nonlinear reversed cone, then the small central cylinder of the lower half of the LH joint, and then a somewhat larger third cylinder in the RH joint. This last device, a convenient method for reducing the oversizing of the lowest twelfths, has been used since by other makers.

4. A dual reverse-conical pattern, with a small barrel leading into a larger reversed cone at the top of the LH joint, was applied by W. Hans Moennig of Philadelphia ca. 1954 to his revised, refraised, and retuned R 13 clarinets. The idea was later used by Anthony Gigliotti for the Selmer 10 G, and it has since been variously adapted in all Selmer soprano clarinets. (See Table I, col. b.) Although most manufacturers now believe that in a thick-walled clarinet the venturi effect of a reverse-conical barrel can focus wind past the lacuna left when the barrel is necessarily pulled out, makers have usually limited such a disparity to barely more than 0.2 mm. in a soprano clarinet. Selmer, however, frequently provides venturi offsets below the barrel which are much larger, and their Recital Series clarinets display an unprecedented linear reduction of as much as 0.75 mm. from top to bottom of the LH joint.

In a wind instrument, some departures from a uniform cylinder or cone are necessary to provide specific corrections of modal ratios and/or improvements of timbre. These variations will not usually benefit other aspects of the instrument's performance. Columns a and b of Table I represent refinements developed in the second half of the twentieth century. While Robert Carrée's polycylindrical bores are adjudged to offer tonal improvement in a smaller bore, the resultant flattening of the R 13 B♭ clarinet's upper third mode requires resorting to some inconvenient fingerings, and this device

Table I

a. Buffet Crampon polycylindrical R 13 B♭, post–1950, barrel and LH joint only.		b. Selmer Recital B♭, with two linear reversed cones, post–1989, barrel and LH joint only.

bore diam., mm.	vertical scale: cm. from top of barrel	bore diam., mm.
14.95	-0-	14.87
	-1-	
	-2-	
14.92	-3-	14.75
14.94	top of LH joint	15.15
	-4-	
14.88	-5-	
14.85	-6-	
	-7-	
	-8-	14.85
	-9-	
14.83	-10-	
14.67	-11-	
14.65	-12-	
14.64	-13-	14.62
	(truncated)	
14.64	-25-	14.38
(length, 25.3 cm.)		(length, 24.9 cm.)

has been beneficially reduced in Buffet Crampon's R 13 A and its Prestige RC models. Selmer's 10 S, 10 G, and Recital clarinets, each of which has a varied version of the maker's two reversed cones, suffer no unusual modal displacements; however, in my opinion the best Boehm clarinet solutions do not abandon but sensibly minimize such proprietary departures, as Yamaha and Leblanc have sought to do. In view of the outstanding timbres and pitches of the Wurlitzer soprano clarinets, which are made without any disjunction of bores from the top of the barrel through a substantially linear cone that decreases to the top of the RH joint, it is difficult to justify for the Boehm any more than quite minimal disjunctions in the bore.

Another caution should be noted: Clarinets with cylinders of almost identical diameters (so that they can be played with the same mouthpiece) ought to be limited to no more than two adjacent pitches. It is little wonder that the clarinet in C remained hardly more than a stepchild during the centuries in which it was made to the same bores as those of the B♭ and A. It is worthwhile noting that in his second version of the R 13 A, Robert Carrée found it better to use a larger cylinder for the RH joint, about 14.75 mm., than the 14.65 mm. of the LH joint. This was a practical if not quite ideal solution to compatibility in the set of two clarinets. Selmer's latest Recital A, on the other hand, now provides a linear reduction to a 14.5 mm. RH joint bore, in contrast to the 14.4 mm. of the Recital B♭.

11

TONE HOLES AND FRAISING

A S MENTIONED EARLIER, the clarinet with unfraised tone holes
was brought to a highly successful design by Henri Selmer between the two World Wars. (In 1993 all of Selmer's soprano clarinets
were fraised, while its E♭ and lower-pitched clarinets were unfraised.)
All soprano clarinets of most makers are still fraised, regardless of
pitch, and so are all oboes and English horns, but not bassoons or
saxophones.

The term applies to a bell-shaped enlargement of a tone hole
above its vertical juncture with the bore, but fraising may also be
accomplished (less satisfactorily) by lowering pad openings or (quite
satisfactorily) as in the French-model flute. Still another kind of
fraising occurs in most clarinets having fraised tone holes and a
smaller bore: an enlargement of the bore above its juncture with
the bell, in order to reduce the modal ratios at the lower end of the
clarinet which have been enlarged by the opening of a speaker vent.
In Benade's words, the following are the effects of fraising:

> In the closed-hole part of a woodwind bore, fraising has the ef-
> fect of increasing the volume enclosed by each altered hole. There
> are three results: (a) the effective bore cross section is increased,
> (b) the sound velocity is decreased so that the frequency is lowered,
> [and] the cutoff frequency is lowered so that a thoroughly fraised
> bore is one which eliminates a few more of the highest components
> in the radiated sound spectrum than is the case with an unfraised
> bore. . . . An instrument with some of the holes unfraised and oth-

ers fraised in varying amounts will have irregular intonation. ["Woodwind Finger Holes," p. 1603.]

In (b) above, although Benade neglects to say so, sound velocity is decreased by fraising, but only in the tone hole's harmonic modes; it is in fact very slightly increased in the fundamental mode when fraising is applied to an existing tone hole. (See further quotation from Benade, below.) Also, while varying the amount of fraising is not ideal, it has to be done frequently, as some tone holes cannot be ideally placed and may be oversized or undersized. For example, in the Buffet Crampon R 13, the D–A hole works when it is practically unfraised, whereas the E–B hole has to be highly fraised. This instrument's specific polycylindricality and the excess venting by several open tone holes below this hole require maximal diminution of the twelfth. (In this regard the Oehler clarinet is superior.)

Benade continues: "Fraising of the open holes has the effect of decreasing their impedance and is equivalent to drilling them through a thinner wall or to enlarging them." This remark further supports my statement that fraising increases fundamental-mode frequencies and decreases upper-mode frequencies as they approach the cutoff frequency of the tone hole. More and more of their energy is dissipated in the open-hole lattice instead of exiting at the fraised first open hole. ("Cutoff frequency" in this case defines the upper limit of a band-pass filter such as a set of open tone holes in a woodwind.)

Quoting further from Benade: "The analysis [of Sec III] implies the cutoff frequency of the open-hole bore is increased by fraising." One finds this conclusion surprising in view of the accepted belief that, in a given bore and regimen of tone holes, fraising produces lower cutoff frequencies. Triébert's Boehm system oboe, ca. 1860 (one of which I have played), is said to have failed because of its large tone holes and brilliant tones. (See Benade, "Characterization of Woodwinds by Tone Hole Cutoff Frequencies," abstract of paper X-3, Bulletin, Acoustical Society of America, 1973.)

In summary, we can make the following conclusions regarding

location, sizing, and fraising of tone holes in a woodwind instrument:

1. The larger the tone hole, the higher its cutoff frequency and the more brilliant its tones. (For example, the Buffet Crampon Prestige RC clarinet achieves fine tonal and intonational balance by slightly enlarging both its tone holes and its bore, as compared with those of the R 13.)

2. The larger the tone hole, the larger its modal frequency ratios.

3. Fraising a tone hole raises its fundamental-mode frequency and decreases its modal frequency ratios. It also effectively enlarges the succeeding bore, which further slows the passage of wind and decreases modal frequency ratios.

4. Fraising a tone hole lowers its cutoff frequency.

5. To the extent that less of the high-frequency harmonic content exits from a tone hole, its output will be perceived as having been emitted from the instrument's bell, and it is therefore more subject to axial projection.

6. The use of smaller bore diameters in soprano clarinets makes the use of fraising mandatory for the achievement of satisfactory intonation.

Effects of Fraising on Performance

The primary purpose of fraising tone holes is to minimize tonal stridency. In the clarinetist's vernacular, it can assist in obtaining a "dark" tone. My great artist-teacher R. M. Arey (who was associated with the Minneapolis Symphony, the Philadelphia Orchestra, the Rochester Philharmonic, and the Eastman School of Music) used an O'Brien crystal mouthpiece for this purpose. But the dimensions of every facet of the instrument may also be manipulated to accomplish this end. Can even a fine performer discern whether another clarinetist is playing a fraised or an unfraised instrument? Probably not, but with the loss of the unfraised soprano clarinet the question is now almost academic.

Since the larger, lower harmony clarinets do not benefit as positively from the tonal enhancement of fraising, one's choice of a bass clarinet should probably depend on its playability without reference to its fraising.

The Practical Limits of Fraising

1. It is advisable to avoid excessively deep, barrel-shaped fraising, as it unduly restricts emission from the hole.

2. Excessively wide fraising causes a loss of integrity in the bore and sacrifices stability. The internal diameter of a fraised hole should not exceed its exterior diameter by more than 30 percent.

3. For best effect with minimal loss of bore surfaces, fraising should be gently concave.

4. The juncture of fraising with the bore should be devoid of any imperfection, since that will cause noise and impair stability.

5. A rounding off of the juncture of bore and fraising will trade off stability for fluency of connection. (As a woodwind is played it usually becomes more flexible.)

6. Fraising of the bore above the bell for the purpose of minimizing the lowest twelfths should be limited to no more than a disjunction of 0.2 mm.; any further fraising of the bore should be moved upward, above the low F♯–C♯ vent, in the interest of maintaining the clarity of the bell tones.

12

FLARE IN THE LOWER BORE
AND THE BELL

Flare in the upper bore of a clarinet is normally limited to the usually linear cone of the mouthpiece. The somewhat exponential flare of the lower joint and bell is necessary for the proper reduction of the lowest twelfths, which have been falsely stretched by the opening of the speaker vent. (In a published article, a prominent music acoustician who is also a bassoonist once seriously questioned the necessity of the clarinet bell!)

While we are aware that the flare of the d'amoré bell of the English horn imparts unique color to its tones, we must be thankful that the d'amoré clarinet bell is no longer with us, since our instrument has so much more timbral unity.

Given a certain bore diameter and a dual-function speaker key, the designer is left with only the conventional devices of adjusting the length and quality of the flare, and properly fraising the tone holes and the flare itself. These operations are interdependent. Small wonder, then, that makers sometimes also take the expedient of slightly enlarging the cylinder of the RH joint to reduce further the lowest twelfths! (But see in Chapter 13 how a single-function speaker vent can improve both timbres and modal ratios.)

Dependence of the Quality of Flare on the
Effective Bore

The size of the enclosed bore chosen for a clarinet in a certain key and the extended scale which it may need to produce determine the length and quality of its flare. The operating rule here is simple: The larger the cylindrical diameter, the better its extreme twelfths and the worse its middle twelfths. With the smaller diameters presently preferred for clarinets, a longer flare becomes necessary for the achievement of useful lower twelfths; and makers are discovering that some fraising usually done just above the bell can frequently be done better around or above the low F♯–C♯ vent. Selmer has successfully used this device as it has reduced the bores of not only its soprano clarinets but also its basset horns and bass clarinets. In its Recital clarinets, the adoption of a full-length LH-joint reversed cone has further corrected the lowest twelfths.

In German-system clarinets, the presence of an alternate vent for low F♯–C♯ in the Oehler clarinet and an auxiliary vent for low G–D in the Reform Boehm actually simplifies the correction of oversized low twelfths. (The present Oehler clarinet avoids a problem by providing two thumb-key vents—for low E and F—thus obtaining marvelous tones and pitches in both registers!)

Extended-range clarinets need the same onset of flare as that used in a standard-range clarinet of the same bore. The same is true for any low D or C clarinet. Particularly with the smaller bores now used, makers are increasingly relying on a double flare as much as on a considerably extended single flare. Makers of low C clarinets know their success (and enjoy it) when they have simultaneously achieved good pitch and good timbre at the low end, and good twelfths overall.

Designs for the Clarinet Bell

The larger bores of the early nineteenth century reappeared in the second quarter of the twentieth century and encouraged in the larger bored, unfraised soprano clarinets of Henri Selmer the revival of Ivan Mueller's strictly conical bell of a century earlier. As Selmer enlarged its soprano clarinet bores after World War I, it properly abandoned its more exponential pattern, only to return to it with its smaller bores. Buffet Crampon has possibly never changed its bell.

The larger the clarinet's bore, the more linear its bell's cone should be. However, even in E. J. Albert's 15 mm. clarinets, the bell produces beautiful tones and pitches with a gently curved bore.

13

CLARINET SPEAKER VENTS AND THE THIRD-LINE B♭

FREQUENCY RATIOS BETWEEN the first two harmonic modes of a closed pipe are more or less radically altered by the inverted hemispheric arc of errors induced in the opening of a speaker vent for the production of harmonic modes, particularly when this vent also functions as a primary producer of the tones of the third-line B♭. These faults prompted a century of searches for methods of separating the speaker function from that for the B♭ (now thoroughly understood) and for methods of reducing frequency ratios mistuned by the dually functioning speaker-B♭ vent, which are still tolerated by those who do not accept any of the several solutions for separate, automatic venting.

Table II, dealing only with modal ratios, does not consider another important advantage of the single-function speaker vent: it enables the production of bell-tone timbres which are nearer to those just above and below, by minimizing the amount of fraising of the bore above the bell which is required in a 14.7 mm. clarinet. The two most important models of Herbert Wurlitzer adopt different means of accomplishing this goal: the Oehler uses auxiliary vents for low E and F; the Reform Boehm has its single-function speaker vent (see Table II).

Table II. Two B♭ Soprano Clarinets, Unlipped Twelfths, Cents
Over- or Undersized

Clarinet A: Dual-function vent, 14.65 mm. bore. Clarinet B: Single-function vent, 14.7 mm. bore, with auxiliary B–F♯–D♯ venting.

Interval (high to low)	Clarinet A	Clarinet B	
G–D, open	+14		
F♯–C♯, 1st finger	+14		
F♯–C♯, side keys	+8		
F–C	+8	+5	
E–B	+9	+4	
E♭–B♭	+6	+3	
D–A	+4	+2	
C♯–G♯	+2	+1	
C–G	+2	+1	
B–F♯, middle finger	-4		
B–F♯, cross key	+3	+3	
B–F♯, auxiliary vent		+1	(with middle finger)
B♭–F	0	-1	
A–E	-1	-2	
A♭–E♭	+3	+1	
G–D	+2		
G–D, auxiliary vent		+1	
F♯–C♯	+7	+3	
F–C	+12	+6	
F–C, with low E♭ ext.	+14	+7	
E–B	+2	+1	
E–B, with low E♭ ext.	+12	+6	

No claim is made as to the accuracy of any single intervallic judgment; their sizes are determined by the bore and the size and location of the speaker vent.

14

THE CLARINET BARREL

IN THEIR EFFECTS on the modal frequency ratios of the clarinet, the mouthpiece and the barrel need to be treated as one variable unit.

With respect to intonation, given a prescribed length, modal ratios supplied by a barrel are determined by the total volume enclosed within it (and the mouthpiece). The larger this area the greater the frequency separation between the upper first and second modes. Also, as detailed in Chapter 9, the farther up a tube an enlargement occurs, the more specifically it affects higher-mode frequencies such as those of the third, fourth, and fifth modes. A pronounced reverse-conical (Moennig) bore in the barrel can therefore raise the upper third-mode pitches slightly while holding down those of the upper second mode.

Tone is complexly affected by the weight of the barrel; the presence or absence of a dually tapered venturi in the barrel; a slight cavity resonance, which may be promoted by a reversed cone in the barrel as well as by another in the LH joint; and the finish of the inner surfaces of the barrel. Less weight produces more brilliant and less massive tones (as is the case with the entire body). The presence or absence of metal rings contributes to this totality.

Flexibility and brilliance will be promoted by the presence of a dually tapered venturi in the barrel, as compared with a linear taper. With the dual taper the upper portion of the bore decreases from a slightly enlarged top to a chosen midpoint, followed by a less rapidly decreasing lower portion.

Wind resistance and wall losses are affected by weight, enclosed volume, and the quality of the inner surfaces.

It is wise to reduce the bore of the barrel slightly when it is lengthened, since the added length provides an increase in a normally enlarged portion of the bore. (Consider a decrease of 0.03 mm. per added millimeter of length.)

15

MOUTHPIECES
Contrasting French and German Designs

I do not use the term "chamber" for either the upper two-thirds or the lower three-fifths of the mouthpiece tube; I have found it less confusing to say that the aperture in the facing called the "window" directs the wind through the compressing "windway" into the mouthpiece's circularly milled "bore." The windway's walls are the "baffle," the two "side walls," and the "short wall." The reed vibrates or beats against the "tip rail" and the two "side rails."

A Comparison of Classical French and German Mouthpieces

	French	German
Tip rail width, minimum	0.6 mm.	0.6 mm.
Width of window at tip	12.0 mm.	11.0 mm.
Width of window at base	8.05 mm.	7.05 mm.
Length of window	31 mm.	31.2 mm.
Side walls of window	straight	straight
Side walls of windway	straight, nearly vertical	straight, widely angling
Windway width, end of baffle	8.15 mm.	10.7 mm.
Curvature of baffle	slightly concave	concave
Length of bore (approximate)	54.0 mm.	56.0 mm.
Total mouthpiece length	89.0 mm.	90.0 mm.

The dimensions in the table are average for professional equipment. The German mouthpiece is usually lighter because of its smaller external circumference; it also has threads and knurls to accommodate a cord ligature.

"Curvature of baffle" refers to its lengthwise pattern, not to the always more or less convex lip below the tip rail, which facilitates the production of high tones. Unlike the three linear walls of the windway, the baffle continues the transverse concavity which it inherits from the radial arc of the tip rail and with which it meets the bore of the mouthpiece. An absolutely straight lengthwise baffle may provide excessive brilliance, whereas an excessively concave baffle may produce an unfocused, dull sound.

Unlike the sometimes circular saxophone windway, the clarinet windway seems always to have been four-sided. With the French mouthpiece, breadth of timbre is obtained by sufficiently widening the window, and tonal focus is then enhanced by keeping the windway's side walls almost vertical. With the German mouthpiece the opposite is true: its narrow window provides focus, but then requires that the side walls angle away from the vertical to obtain breadth for its tones.

Although a clarinet mouthpiece could be made to play in tune with a strictly cylindrical bore, the customary practice of having the largest perturbation of the clarinet's bore either in the barrel or just below it makes a cone advisable. (Not even the otherwise cylindrical bore of the Boosey & Hawkes 1010 could completely eliminate this cone.)

Control of the total volume enclosed by the mouthpiece is essential to its presentation of good modal ratios for the upper twelfths. To bring up flat throat tones without correspondingly raising upper clarion tones, one should try first using a smaller-bored barrel, then perhaps a barrel that is both smaller and shorter. A last, lifesaving resort for the mouthpiece can be to remove one or two millimeters from the tenon and the shoulder above it.

Prevailing needs for perhaps three classes of ensembles in which a player may participate may determine whether the performer uses a close, medium, or open mouthpiece facing. Tradition deems that the Boehm clarinetist will use a mouthpiece with a wider window and a shorter, more open facing than that needed for the German mouthpiece, with its narrow window and longer, closer facing. However, when proper dimensions are given for the bore and the windway, these designs can be made to play equally well with either system.

A mouthpiece of intermediate design was widely used in the first half of the twentieth century, and it may be seen again. I have such a mouthpiece, made for a 15 mm. clarinet, ca. 1920, possibly by Frank L. Kaspar, in Goldbeck's Chicago establishment. It has a table of solid gold, a nickel silver bore and windway, and a hard rubber body, all put together with marvelous dimensions which place it at a midpoint between the German and French designs. (It had to be shortened 2 mm. to make it suitable for a 14.65 mm. clarinet with a Moennig reversed-cone barrel.) W. Hans Moennig probably developed his sharply reducing barrel bore to enable similar mouthpieces to be played with our smaller-bored clarinets.

Various devices and kits for measurement and adjustment of mouthpiece facings have been available in Europe and in the United States, which has been slow to adopt metric measurements (1 in. = 2.54 cm.). For the soprano clarinet, thickness gauges may be assembled as listed in the following chart.

Typical French and German Orchestral Clarinet Facings

Gauges used:	Tip	0.9 mm.	0.6 mm.	0.25 mm.	0.04 mm.
		.035 in.	.024 in.	.01 in.	.0015 in.

For these facings the above gauges will stop at about:

French facing:	1.12 mm.	2.8 mm.	5.8 mm.	11.5 mm.	17.5 mm.
German facing:	1.01 mm.	2 mm.	5.6 mm.	12.5 mm.	21 mm.

The tip rail needs to be no wider than 1 mm. For greatest endurance of the reed, the side rails should extend outward for the full width of the reed, although some players prefer the clarity and lower noise level of narrower side rails. (Such judgments are not readily supportable by spectral analysis.)

The German practice throughout the twentieth century has followed Oskar Oehler's development of a lengthwise concave table for the reed, which is now found on some French mouthpieces, including Vandoren's. With the longer, closer facing and the string ligature of the German mouthpiece, the concavity of about 0.03 mm.

usually found in the table can provide somewhat greater flexibility. Its superiority for the French mouthpiece is less conclusive, though when it is not overdone (as is often the case) it is worthwhile. There is also a reasonable logic for a minuscule transverse concavity of the table, since reeds always dry with a comparable convexity, but this should be almost immeasurable if done at all.

16

ALTERNATIVE MECHANISMS
AND SYSTEMS

The German Clarinet

AT THE BEGINNING of the twentieth century, Oskar Oehler, at first a member of the Berlin Philharmonic, took an instrument which lacked some of the mobility of the Boehm clarinet and brought it to an equal, if slightly different, capability. It was his adaptation of the F-resonance mechanism of the oboe which provided a solution to the one remaining serious weakness of the German clarinet, the lack of an in-tune alternative to the standard cross-key B♭–F.

After World War II the pursuit of excellence for the Oehler clarinet was carried on by Fritz Wurlitzer, and then his son Herbert, at Neustadt-Aisch. The demand for smaller bores, initiated by Robert Carrée of Buffet Crampon in 1950, led to their adoption by the German makers, who settled on a soprano size of about 14.7 mm. This made advisable the addition of a thumb-key leverage to control resonance venting for the low E and F, which would otherwise be flatter in the new bore. No other significant improvements have been applied to the Oehler clarinet in the second half of the twentieth century. The great virtue of the thumb-key is that it provides for these notes in each mode the very best, no-compromise timbres and pitches, whereas in the smaller-bored Boehm system both have been compromised a bit. (An exception is the low F-resonance vent available for the Selmer Recital clarinets.)

The Full-Boehm Clarinet

After 150 years, the creation of Louis-Auguste Buffet and H. Klosé, the "Boehm Ordinaire" of seventeen keys and six rings, remains quite near its original essence. The standard extra mechanisms of the improved and full-Boehm models throughout the twentieth century have been the seventh ring, for trills and a good forked E♭–B♭ on the left hand; the articulated B–F♯ whole-step trill as performed while holding down the C♯–G♯ key and trilling with the middle finger of the right hand; the RH duplicate C♯–G♯ key; the LH A♭–E♭ key; and the low E♭ extension and its key. In the theatre orchestra of the early twentieth century, the full Boehm became the only clarinet carried by most professionals, and it still may be heard in the opera orchestras of the world. With the articulated C♯–G♯ one loses the long, closed high F while gaining better intonation and tone for each of the hole's registers. With the seventh ring one loses a good high F–G trill. The low E♭–B♭ provides good trills in both registers, although its B♭ may not be tolerable for sustained tones. While this mechanism offers other useful fingerings, and for the transposer and doubler it has been indispensable, it is now becoming rare.

The Mazzeo System Soprano Clarinets

By far the most successful special-system clarinet of the twentieth century (aside from the standard full-Boehm models) has been that of Rosario Mazzeo. In it the first finger of the left hand retains its A and A♭ functions, while B♭ is produced with the A key in conjunction with one or more of the RH finger rings, a leverage which always provides proper speaker sizing and excellent B♭ tones. An exceptional fingering not otherwise available has been an articulated E–B to F♯–C♯ trill mechanism providing correct pitches and tones on F♯–C♯ when the E–B key is held. The Mazzeo System was available from Selmer ca. 1955–1985 but most clarinetists were unwilling to learn a different fingering for third-line B♭.

The Schmidt-Wurlitzer Reform Boehm (previously described), with its auxiliary venting for B♭, its small speaker vent, its B–F♯–D♯ resonance mechanism, and its special A♭ trill mechanism, has survived for much of the twentieth century, though it is quite expensive and rare. Its devices have made it one of the best-tuned clarinets available, along with the similar, but not identical, Yamaha German Boehm.

17

REEDS AND LIGATURES

Reeds

A STUDY OF THE dimensions of a variety of mouthpieces reveals that they have been made not only in the extremes of each of the two classical types but also in another which effectively compromises the dimensions of each (see Chapter 15). Ideally, then, there is already a need for a reed to fit such a mouthpiece, although some clarinetists are using those designed for the German mouthpiece on French mouthpieces.

For the German soprano clarinet mouthpiece, the reed is typically about 66 mm. long, and for the French it is usually 68 mm. long. However, since a good piece of cane is frequently worth reworking, 68 mm. ought to be equally good for the German mouthpiece.

How thick should the finished base of the soprano clarinet reed be? After some years of urging by clarinetists, manufacturers who formerly saved all thicker cane for saxophone reeds have recognized that clarinet reeds also need greater thickness to help resist collapse. Even after cane has been well seasoned, its very hard outer surface retains its length while the softer interior fiber continues to shrink; and, as the masters of handmade reeds have long known, the base of a clarinet reed needs to be a minimum of 3 mm. in finished thickness to be durable.

In 1978 I entered the office of the world's largest manufacturer of single reeds to make this and other suggestions for clarinet reeds. They were courteously received, and in 1988 I was invited to supervise the design of a new clarinet reed, which by 1993 was the corporation's all-time most successful reed.

For the width of the reed, we can safely take Vandoren's standard, about 13.05 mm. at the tip and 11.55 mm. at the base. The Olivieri reed, with a wide tip, a thick, narrow base, and a length of 69 mm., is an exception which I believe to be unnecessarily wide at the tip. Since the German mouthpiece has a window which may be 1 mm. narrower at the tip, the German reed is also narrower, about 12.7 mm. at the tip. It is interesting to note that in 1981 the Chinese, whose musical traditions were established under British influence, still preferred large-bore clarinets having mouthpieces with a wide window, for which their clarinetists all made their own excellent and unusually wide reeds.

The term "vamp," which is derived from the shoe, is the name commonly given to the vibrating, tapered, and variably arched blade of the reed. For the German mouthpiece, with its narrow window and longer, closer facing, the reed is narrower and thicker, with a less-arched vamp, and it can produce relatively cool, dark tones which become more brilliant as the facing is opened and the reed is softened. For the classical French mouthpiece, the reed customarily has a higher-arched vamp with somewhat thinner sides and tip, with which the tones produced are expected to be warmer or more brilliant.

As to the logic of the vamp and the mouthpiece facing:

1. The thicker reed needed for a long, close facing favors the production of lower partials, and vice versa.

2. The higher-arched reed needed for the wider window of the French mouthpiece achieves its responsiveness with a thinner tip and sides, and it favors the production of higher partials. There is some latitude available for those who prefer the slightly darker tones of the reed with thicker sides.

3. There is no theoretical support for a practice which has afflicted the production of most makers of reeds for the French mouthpiece for many years: a very short vamp, below which occurs an unneces-

sarily wide and deep surface cut. This device, which probably origi-
nated as an attempt to improve uniformity of grading of reeds having insufficiently thick bases, is destructive to the vibratory character
of the reed. It no longer appears in the best of today's reeds, of
which the Vandoren V 12 and Black Master (German) reeds are representative, nor did it appear in any of Vandoren's pre–World War
II reeds. The same is true of the Olivieri reed. For the soprano clarinet, a 34 mm. vamp and an absolutely minimal surface cut on a 3+
mm. base are ideal and provide longer life.

The tightly closed reed case in which a reed is stored against an
impervious plate is admittedly the most convenient method for
keeping a reed ready for immediate use. However, one who wishes
to save a good reed for later use should place it in a flat, well-venti-
lated open-air holder, such as the Vandoren plastic clarinet reed
holder, which effectively minimizes decay and typically doubles or
quadruples the life of a reed.

Ligatures

The German mouthpiece, with its 22 milled channels and two
knurls for a strong knitted cord, is well designed to hold the reed
in place. The rest of the world, however, has long since concluded
that a ligature serves adequately and conveniently. For most of us
the one unforgivable sin is the failure of a ligature to hold the reed's
position when the mouthpiece is removed.

Two heavy, soft nickel silver ligatures with screws over the reed
have served me a lifetime without slipping. This metal slightly
damps high frequencies. Players who prefer less damping may be
happier with a lighter nickel silver or the still more brilliant sounds
of the brass ligatures currently supplied by most makers. Plastic ligatures may absorb some high-frequency vibration, as perhaps does
the German cord.

In the second half of the twentieth century, a belief has emerged
that a reed will play more freely if it is held by a ligature which
provides limited pressure points rather than a complete envelop-

ment. To the extent that the reed is held in this manner it may play more strongly and with greater brilliance. Certainly any ligature does this when it is moved toward the base of the reed. The Rovner single-screw impregnated woven fabric ligature is the most convenient I have used.

Every device and material used in a ligature offers its own characteristics, though they mean far more to the player than to the listener. Again, confidence in the product is the player's prime consideration.

APPENDIX A
A Summary of Clarinet Acoustics

ACOUSTICAL PRINCIPLES PERTAIN equally to clarinets in all pitches. However, sopranino, soprano, alto, basset, bass, and the contra clarinets all have differing tonal and intonational needs. They have more or less strictly cylindrical bores; some have fraising; and all have mechanisms which are individually appropriate. Principles are constant; needs vary. For example, Selmer, which pioneered the unfraised clarinet, in 1993 supplied only its sopranos with fraised tone holes. This review relates the dimensions and materials of clarinets to their performance and provides an abbreviated manual of practical acoustics for the player.

Dimensions and Tone

For a clarinet designed at a given pitch, the larger its bore the mellower and blander its tones will be. Since a larger bore must have larger tone holes to produce registers which may be played in tune, it will also be less resistive. Further, it is less likely to have fraised tone holes, as they are more appropriate to smaller bores.

Departures from a purely cylindrical bore will increase or decrease formant resonances within certain frequency bands, according to their location and shape; e.g., the polycylindrical bore of the LH half of the Buffet Crampon R 13, which produces a mezzo-soprano band that is more characteristic of a larger bore; the bell of a woodwind, which pronouncedly affects the timbres of tones near it; and the d'amoré bell of the English horn and the former clarinet d'amoré, with their idiosyncratic mellowness. Fraising (undercutting) of tone holes reduces emission of high frequencies and effectively enlarges the instrument's bore. The Oehler-system clarinet, which for a given bore size seems to tolerate more fraising than does the Boehm clarinet, is therefore known for its slightly darker tones, to which the German mouthpiece may also contribute.

Materials and Tone

In 1925, metal clarinets seemed destined to replace those of wood. In 1928, I heard a concert by the U.S. Army Band in which the entire soprano clarinet section consisted of metal instruments; the section tone was limpid and beautiful. That we no longer have metal clarinets is probably because metal does not adapt to fraising of tone holes. (In spite of their conviction that they hear and feel a more vibrant, woody tone when playing a wooden clarinet, in numerous trials even the best players have been unable to identify consistently the material involved.)

Thicker, heavier wooden walls increase lower-frequency resonances, and to the performer, at least, a lighter, thinner-walled blackwood clarinet almost always seems to have more of the brilliance of a coloratura soprano tone. The relative softness of Baroque and early Classical woodwind sounds was in part due to damping of their tones by their less dense and more absorbent boxwood walls, and in part due to the lower admittances of wind, which resulted from their small, fraised tone holes.

Dimensions and Pitch

There is an inverse relationship between a wind instrument's size of bore and its modal frequency ratios. Perhaps it is just as well that players have not always recognized this! In symphony orchestras and chamber music (usually with mouthpieces having closer facings), bores close to 14.65 mm. are presently preferred, whereas jazz players, who use more open facings, frequently like a bore close to 15 mm.

Three areas of departure from a cylindrical bore are common to almost all clarinets: a slightly conical bore in the mouthpiece; a reversed cone in the barrel or the metal neck, which takes its place in alto, bass, and contra alto and contra bass clarinets; and a curvilinear, partly exponential enlargement in the lowest third of a clarinet's bore.

Many soprano clarinets with bores close to 15 mm. were formerly made with no appreciable reversed-conical enlargement of the LH joint. At the end of the twentieth century, all soprano clarinets incorporate one or more of a variety of reversed cones in the bore of the LH joint. This is the part of the bore in which our leading manufacturers are still stubbornly individualistic.

Rules for Perturbations (Departures) from a Strict Cylinder

An enlargement of bore in the mouthpiece increases upper modal ratios most; such increases diminish toward the lower end of the tube. An enlargement of bore in the barrel increases the frequency ratios of the upper twelfths. A reversed conical enlargement in the LH joint increases upper- to middle-twelfth ratios. A cylindrical enlargement in the upper half of the LH joint increases middle twelfth ratios and decreases upper third-mode ratios. In a highly decreasing linear reverse-conical LH joint bore, the modal ratios assume the sizes normally expected from the mean bore area.

Frequency Displacements by Speaker Vents

Second-mode displacements produced by opening the speaker vent cannot be eliminated by perturbations of bore, though they may be minimized. (The size of the B♭–F twelfth at the displacement null of the open speaker vent is almost entirely dependent on the mean diameter of the middle third of a clarinet's bore.)

Tone Hole Sizes

For a given location, increased tone-hole size raises emitted frequencies in each mode, increases ratios between first-mode and higher-mode frequencies, and produces more brilliant tones as the hole's cutoff frequency is raised and less high-frequency energy is lost in the open-hole bore.

Fraising

Fraising of a tone hole raises its first-mode frequency, decreases the frequency ratios of tones emitted from this hole, and produces less brilliant tones as the hole's cutoff frequency is lowered. Fraising of excessive width and/or depth destroys stability and clarity of tones. Until Boehm perfected his cylindrically bored flute almost all woodwind instruments had fraised tone holes. Among the first soprano clarinets to abandon fraising were those made by Henri Selmer after World War I, and by 1925 he had brought this genre to its highest state. Following the appearance of Robert Carrée's new Buffet Crampon R 13 in 1950, the world rediscovered the tonal virtues of a smaller-bored instrument with fraised tone holes.

At the end of the twentieth century, the clarinet has finally approached a state of acoustical advancement comparable to that reached in 1650 by the Cremonese violin makers who were Antonio Stradivari's immediate predecessors. I predict that there will be such a maker of Boehm clarinets.

APPENDIX B
Tonal Formants in Clarinets

ASIDE FROM THE exchangeable mouthpiece and reed, the factors which affect areas of spectral emphasis (tonal formants) may be listed as follows:

1. Density and total weight of the body (exclusive of its mechanism, which we presume to have been made no heavier than necessary for its strength and durability): For a given bore, a small change in body weight will produce a just-noticeable difference in its overall formant color. Increased weight of the body demands greater absorption of wind pressure by the instrument's walls. Increased weight in the bell affects performance and color in the region near it, whereas a heavier barrel (including its metal rings, if present), has its formant effect on all tones. For example, Buffet Crampon's thinner-walled Elite has a soprano color, while its R 13, with an essentially identical bore but a heavier body with metal joint rings, has a mezzo-soprano or contralto color.

2. Bore size: While the basic cylinder is sized to control its modal ratios, formant color is also tied to the enclosed volume—the smaller the enclosed volume the more brilliant its emitted tones.

3. Departures from an essentially cylindrical tube: To the extent that they are specifically applied, they will affect formant color. Perhaps even before 1918, Henri Selmer led in the now complete abandonment of the strictly cylindrical LH joint of the clarinet, in which a long reversed cone sufficiently mellowed its tonal formant to enable him to discard fraising. Also, in 1949, Robert Carrée developed his specifically polycylindrical LH joint, whose cavity resonance made possible a mellower formant in a smaller bore.

Important Models (1993)

The Wurlitzer Oehler clarinet achieves a quite mellow tonal formant with a 14.7 mm. cylinder, a linear reversed cone from the top of the barrel to the center joint, heavy fraising, and extra bore length above the bell, made possible by its resonance vents for low E and F. Among European clarinetists the Wurlitzer Reform Boehm is widely acclaimed, though I do not find its formant color identical to that of the Wurlitzer Oehler.

Since 1955 Buffet Crampon's R 13s have been the most widely played clarinet ever made, chiefly because of their mellow formant in a smaller bore. In France this firm's 14.71 mm. Prestige RC clarinets, with a slightly reduced polycylindricality and 442 Hz pitches, are preferred. G. Leblanc's 1990 14.65 mm. sopranos (Opus, Concerto, and Infinité) and the Yamaha models after 1975 have all been modeled after the R 13. Each of these achieves slightly better third-mode pitches in the B♭ clarinet, while perhaps not quite duplicating the formant of the R 13.

Selmer's present three soprano clarinet models do not aspire to duplicate the R 13; instead, their approach to a mellower formant concentrates on different versions of double reversed cones in the ca. 14.4 mm. Recital, the 14.65 mm. 10 S, and the 14.71 mm. 10 G, with the Recital having a heavier body.

We look forward to a time when these quite disparate designs can be reconciled into one best solution. We really do want to play together, don't we?

APPENDIX C
Mouthpieces: Beware of the Bore

A T HAND ARE two soprano clarinet mouthpieces, each having
what might appear to be standard dimensions. They are an Ed-
die Daniels, without a facing name or number; and a Riffault Su-
perfini R M, No. N4. Both were purchased in 1992 from a reputable
supplier, and each came with a relatively moderate facing. The
Daniels is well designed for today's clarinets, although its interior
finish is typical of the molded and unpolished surfaces now found
in most commercial production. The Riffault still has the carefully
finished interior typical of the best clarinet mouthpiece.

But what of the dimensions of the Riffault? (I believe it is not
one of their current production.) Aside from the need for a windway
which will provide enough focus for secure production of high
tones, the most critical dimension is its total enclosed volume, which
must provide a match for the reversed conical and cylindrical volume
of the remainder of the instrument. While a larger mouthpiece bore
can be shortened so as to provide a proper volume, experience leads
to the conclusion that performance will be more secure if correct
conicity and length of bore are maintained with the right volume.
There is some latitude in the division of the mouthpiece's length
between windway and bore; if the bore is longer the windway
should be smaller, but the volume must be maintained (see the Vandoren crystal mouthpiece). The following are the bore dimensions
of the Daniels and the Riffault (their total length is similar, ca. 89
mm.):

	Daniels	Riffault
Length of bore at juncture of windway	54 mm.	56 mm.
Diameter at 4 cm. above base	14.71 mm.	14.89 mm.
Diameter at base of bore	14.91 mm.	14.96 mm.
Depth of windway from base of window	13.5 mm.	14.5 mm.

Benade has given an equivalent volume for a B♭ soprano clarinet mouthpiece enclosure of 13.25 cu. cm., which referred to the volume suitable for a tube close to 15 mm. rather than for the now more typical 14.65 mm. clarinet (*Fundamentals of Musical Acoustics*, p. 472). The Daniels mouthpiece has excellent modal ratios for the 14.65 mm. bores, whereas one questions whether this Riffault would be playable with a bore of less than 15.1 mm. Minor corrections of modal ratios can of course be made by changing barrel bores.

The width of the window affects the strength of a reed appropriate for a given facing. While the long, close German facing demands a thicker reed, this need is moderated by a narrower window. The window of the Riffault, being wider than average, requires a slightly stronger reed than that of the Daniels.

The area enclosed in the windway critically affects performability and pitch in the upper modes, flexibility vs. stability, and overall timbres. The top quarter of the baffle should be slightly convex and the remaining three quarters slightly concave. Given a window 31 mm. long, a line drawn vertically to the baffle from the bottom of the window should measure between 13+ mm. and 14+ mm.

For greater detail see Chapter 15.

APPENDIX D
Fine-tuning the Clarinet

Mouthpieces and Barrels

ASIDE FROM A properly shaped window, a facing which encour-
ages the best embouchure for the player, a windway which provides good focus and color, a finely finished interior surface, and a
defect-free joining with the mouthpiece bore, an indispensable fea-
ture of the mouthpiece is a bore which contains a proper volume.
When smaller-bored clarinets became popular after 1950, many of
the best makers did not reduce the mouthpiece bore, and W. Hans
Moennig of Philadelphia pioneered the use of a smaller reversed
cone in the bore of the barrel to control oversizing of the upper
twelfths.

Tuning Rings and Barrels

Rings can provide a risky short-term solution for space left when
tuning downward. One must carry two lengths of barrel and hope
that no more than 1 mm. of pullout space will be necessary during
the service. Selmer's thinnest tuning ring can be quickly filed to fit
in the center joint, but one must make one's own tool for retrieving
it when necessary. It is widely believed that the vortex of a reversed
cone can reduce distress when space is left below it. (Selmer has led
in this practice.) Ideally, for each extra millimeter of added barrel
length one should reduce the bore by perhaps 0.03 mm. to retain
similar modal relationships.

Pad Openings

Decreasing pad clearance lowers pitches in each register, increases
wind resistance, reduces high-frequency emission, and lowers upper-

mode pitches more than first-mode pitches. Decreasing pad clearance effectively increases fraising.

Adjusting Tone Holes

The measurement of tone hole diameters is complicated by the varied practices of different makers. Buffet Crampon provides conical tone holes, while most other makers' are cylindrical. The application of tape increases fraising. A tone hole which has been excessively fraised or enlarged can be repaired with epoxy or nail polish. Excess epoxy must be removed within four hours; excess nail polish continues its shrinkage for days. (I well remember seeing nail polish in the tone holes of Reginald Kell's clarinets.) If a tone hole is insufficiently fraised but not too large, one may use a file such as a Nicholson 6 in. (15 cm.) extra-fine #2 crossing Swiss pattern file (the sharp end should be smoothly rounded). The cardinal rules are to limit the filing stroke to one angle only, about 20° away from the vertical; to press very lightly when filing into the bore; to maintain a uniformly round fraised hole; not to round off the fraised wall into the bore; and to remember that there was probably a reason why the maker did not do this in the first place!

APPENDIX E
Stability, Flexibility, and Response in Clarinets

AMONG THE WIND instruments, the clarinet and the double reeds are the most critical in their setting of an appropriate balance between stability and flexibility. Wooden instruments become less stable as they swell, warp, shrink, and sometimes crack in spite of the best of care. Over the years, wearing of the exterior of tone holes may raise pitches, and the gradual erosion of the inner edges of tone holes may also alter an instrument's original stability—all of which may contribute to a player's conclusion that the instrument's pristine stability has departed. Of course there may be another reason: the clarinet is only now reaching a quality of design comparable to that of the flute in 1850.

Throughout the bore, linear dimensions promote stability, while nonlinear and curved perturbations provide flexibility. Convex fraising of tone holes and rounding off of tone-hole junctures with the bore also increase flexibility and demand more precise control. Gently concave fraising, which is now standard (with some variation), is believed to provide the best tones with adequate control.

Hidden interstices between the joints of a clarinet can impair its intonation and response. The best makers set a precise standard in this matter; built-in gaps should never exceed 0.2 mm. in a soprano clarinet. Dual-purpose vents, such as the LH F–C finger hole of the Boehm clarinet, can affect the quality of passage from one mode to another as well as the security of the upper mode. The size of this vent is critical, and so is the amount of fraising. The soprano clarinet might very well benefit from the presence of the oboe's vented platen; most of us cover the ring and hole in this manner quite frequently, particularly if this vent needs more fraising. (Consider, for instance, Prokofiev's pianissimo E♭ to high E♭ octave slur in his Piano Concerto No. 3, or, with the B♭ clarinet, D to D.)

The quality of the interior surfaces and the acoustical regularity of the bore are foremost determinants of responsiveness. The presence of too many vents in a bore damages response, à la ocarina! For that matter, the greater the number of tone holes, the less fraising a clarinet should have.

APPENDIX F
Contemporary Standards for Modal Ratios in Clarinets

AT THE END of the twentieth century there are two sets of definitive pitch standards for the soprano clarinet:

One is obtainable with a dual-purpose speaker vent, i.e., a vent which serves in the Boehm system to produce third-line B♭ with the addition of the A and A♭ vents; by itself to produce second-mode high D; and, with the appropriate keys and holes covered, to produce each of the other tones of the second-mode chromatic scale. In conjunction with the opening of one or more additional register vents, this speaker vent continues to serve for most fingerings of tones in the third, fourth, and fifth modes.

The other is obtainable with any of three mechanisms which separate the speaker and the B♭ vent functions. At present, only one of these mechanisms is produced in a factory—the auxiliary venting mechanism of the Wurlitzer Reform Boehm System and the Yamaha German Boehm, which uses a properly sized speaker vent to which is added the A key, an auxiliary vent for B♭, and, if desired, also the A♭ key. The remaining options are vent-exchange mechanisms: one in which a lever activated by the open A key closes the speaker vent and opens a B♭ vent (a mechanism apparently first developed for the Oehler clarinet by Georg Graessel of Nuremberg in 1919 and subsequently redone by Georges Leblanc for his Boehm clarinets); and Rosario Mazzeo's mechanism for his Boehm system, in which the rings of the right hand open the well-placed B♭ vent when the speaker key is not pressed. The Kaspar-Stubbins mechanism, which provided auxiliary venting for a small speaker vent in the manner of the Reform Boehm, was at one time produced by Noblet, while Selmer's Omega clarinet of ca. 1950 used an exchange mechanism. Expensive custom installation of some of these mechanisms is still available. On the whole, the auxiliary venting systems are perhaps more dependable, and they are presently the only factory options.

In any of these mechanisms the speaker vent can be independently sized to produce the best-placed twelfths and third-mode pitches. (In the first Yamaha German Boehms I found the size of the speaker vent a bit small for both the upper twelfths and the third mode; this was easily corrected, of course.) Both the Wurlitzer and the Yamaha include auxiliary venting for the middle-finger B–F$\sharp$–D$\sharp$, which is a perfect solution in each register. With either clarinet, oversized twelfths are virtually eliminated, and sharp upper mode fingerings are less sharp (see Table II, p. 48).

Unlike the speaker-B$\flat$ vent exchange mechanisms applied to the soprano clarinet, those for the bass clarinet usually serve also as a speaker vent for the lowest fourth of the second mode. The value of an additional speaker vent system as an improvement for the soprano clarinet has been explored in the Marchi clarinet developed by Selmer. Is there a place for one of these ideas in the soprano clarinet of the future?

BIBLIOGRAPHY

Backus, John. *The Acoustical Foundations of Music*, 2d ed. New York: W. W. Norton, 1977.

Baines, Anthony. *Woodwind Instruments and Their History*. New York: W. W. Norton, 1957.

Bate, Philip. *The Oboe: An Outline of Its History, Development, and Construction*, 3d ed. New York: W. W. Norton, 1975.

———. *The Flute: A Study of Its History, Development, and Construction*, 2d ed. New York: W. W. Norton, 1979.

Benade, Arthur H. "On Woodwind Instrument Bores." *Journal of the Acoustical Society of America* 31 (February 1959):137–46.

———. "On the Mathematical Theory of Woodwind Finger Holes." *Journal of the Acoustical Society of America* 32 (December 1960): 1591–1608. Reprinted in *Benchmark Papers in Acoustics*, New York: Halstead Press, John Wiley & Sons, 1977.

———. "Characterization of Woodwinds by Tone Hole Cutoff Frequencies." Paper read at the spring 1973 meeting of the Acoustical Society of America.

———. *Fundamentals of Musical Acoustics*. New York: Oxford University Press, 1976. 2d ed., revised by the author, Mineola, N.Y.: Dover Publications, 1990.

———. "The Physics of a New Clarinet Design." Unpublished paper, Western Reserve University, Cleveland, 1980.

———. "On the Tuning of Clarinets." Unpublished paper, n.d.

Brymer, Jack. *Clarinet*. London: MacDonald and Jane's Publishers Ltd., 1976.

Gibson, O. Lee. "Claranalysis." *The Clarinet*: 1–20 (1973–1993) [analytic studies of the instrument].

———. "The Ear as an Analyzer of Musical Tones." *The Clarinet* 5/2 (1978):8–11.

Kroll, Oskar. *The Clarinet*, rev. ed., translated by Hilda Morris. New York: Taplinger Publishing Co., 1968.

Mazzeo, Rosario. *The Clarinet: Excellence and Artistry*. Sherman Oaks, Cal.: Alfred Publishing Co., 1981.

Pino, David. *The Clarinet and Clarinet Playing*. New York: Charles Scribner's Sons, 1980.

Rendall, F. Geoffrey. *The Clarinet*, 3d ed., revised by Philip Bate. New York: W. W. Norton, 1971.

Stubbins, William H. *The Art of Clarinetistry: The Acoustical Mechanism of the Clarinet as a Basis for the Art of Music Performance*, 2d ed. Ann Arbor, Mich.: Ann Arbor Publishers, 1965.

Weston, Pamela. *Clarinet Virtuosi of the Past*. Amersham, Buckinghamshire, England: Halstan & Co. Ltd., 1971.

———. *More Clarinet Virtuosi of the Past*. Amersham, Buckinghamshire, England: Halstan & Co. Ltd., 1977.

Worman, Walter E. "Self-Sustained Nonlinear Oscillations of Medium Amplitude in Clarinet-Like Systems." Diss., Case Western Reserve University, 1971.

INDEX

ABS plastics, 23
Africa: woods and manufacture, 15
Albert, E. J., 6, 7, 11, 46
Albert, Eugene, 11
Albert, J. B., 11
Albert, Jacques Lucien, 11
Albert clarinets: Mueller-Albert system, 6, 24, 34. *See also* Germany, German-system clarinets
Alexander's New York catalog, 10
altitude, effects on instruments, 27
Arey, R. M., 11, 42
Aspen Music School, 8
Australia and New Zealand: clarinetists, 15
Austria: manufacturers, 12
auxiliary vents, 57
axial projection, 42

Backus, John, 17–18, 19
baffle: defined, 21; shapes of, 52
barrel: effect on modal frequency ratios, 49; effect on tone, 49; and LH joint, 32; reverse-conical enlargement, 32
Barret system, 10
bass clarinet, 23, 43
bassoon, 2
Bates, Earl, 8
Belgium: clarinet makers, 11
bell: d'amoré (English horn), 44; shapes, 45, 46
Bellison, Simeon, 7
Benade, Arthur H., vii, 33, 70; on acoustical principles, 19; on effects of fraising, 40–41; on frequency determination, 30; on adjusting frequency ratios, 31; on materials, 24

Bettoney, Harry, 14
Black Master (reed), 60
Bloch, Kalman, 4
body materials: ABS plastics, 23; importance of to player vs. listener, 23, 24; metals, 3, 23, 64; woods, 22. *See also* metal clarinets
Boehm, Theobald, 2, 3, 28
Boehm clarinets, 4, 5, 11, 12, 28; unfraised, 32; vents, 45, 75. *See also* Reform Boehm clarinet
Bonade, Daniel, 8
Boosey & Hawkes, 8, 12; 1010 model clarinet, 12, 29, 34, 36, 52
bore, 28–30; diameter, 38; effective area, 21; enlarged lower third, 64–65; enlarged upper half LH joint, 32; large-bore clarinets, 8–9; minimizing disjunctions in, 38; and mouthpieces, 21, 31–32, 64, 69–70; perturbations of, 30, 64–65; reducing gaps in, 27; terminology, 20; types, 36–37; venturi bore, 33. *See also* perturbations
—size: effect on formants, 67; and flexibility and stability, 73; in jazz, 30, 64; and national styles, 11, 12, 13; ratios, 29; vs. weight, 24–25
Briccialdi, B♭ thumb lever, 2
Brod and Triébert, 2
Brussels Conservatory, 3
Brymer, Jack, 8, 29
Buffet, Louis-Auguste, 28, 56; and Boehm-system clarinet, 10; and French-system bassoon, 2; developer of moveable rings, 3, 28
Buffet Crampon, 2, 10, 11, 12, 15, 29; 15.65 mm. clarinet, 24; 435 Hz B♭

O. LEE GIBSON is Professor Emeritus of Music at the University of North Texas, the Founding Editor of *The Clarinet*, and a past president of the International Clarinet Society.